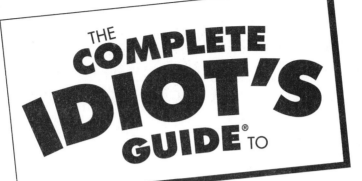

THE
COMPLETE
IDIOT'S
GUIDE® TO

Self-Testing
Your IQ

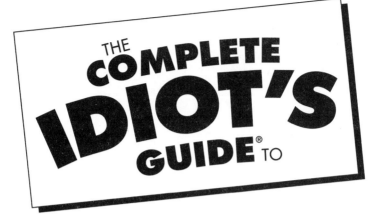

Self-Testing Your IQ

by Dr. Jean Cirillo

ALPHA

A member of Penguin Group (USA) Inc.

ALPHA BOOKS

Published by the Penguin Group

Penguin Group (USA) Inc., 375 Hudson Street, New York, New York 10014, USA

Penguin Group (Canada), 90 Eglinton Avenue East, Suite 700, Toronto, Ontario M4P 2Y3, Canada (a division of Pearson Penguin Canada Inc.)

Penguin Books Ltd., 80 Strand, London WC2R 0RL, England

Penguin Ireland, 25 St. Stephen's Green, Dublin 2, Ireland (a division of Penguin Books Ltd.)

Penguin Group (Australia), 250 Camberwell Road, Camberwell, Victoria 3124, Australia (a division of Pearson Australia Group Pty. Ltd.)

Penguin Books India Pvt. Ltd., 11 Community Centre, Panchsheel Park, New Delhi—110 017, India

Penguin Group (NZ), 67 Apollo Drive, Rosedale, North Shore, Auckland 1311, New Zealand (a division of Pearson New Zealand Ltd.)

Penguin Books (South Africa) (Pty.) Ltd., 24 Sturdee Avenue, Rosebank, Johannesburg 2196, South Africa

Penguin Books Ltd., Registered Offices: 80 Strand, London WC2R 0RL, England

Publisher: *Marie Butler-Knight*
Editorial Director: *Mike Sanders*
Senior Managing Editor: *Billy Fields*
Acquisitions Editor: *Michele Wells*
Development Editor: *Michael Thomas*

Production Editor: *Kayla Dugger*
Copy Editor: *Lisanne V. Jensen*
Cover and Book Designer: *Bill Thomas*
Layout: *Ayanna Lacey*
Proofreader: *Laura Caddell*

Contents at a Glance

Appendixes

Contents

Appendixes

Introduction

Have you ever wondered how smart you really are? Of course you have. We already know that you are smarter than at least 20 percent of the world's population. How can I make that statement without knowing you, however? It's simple. You wouldn't be reading this book otherwise. The fact that you were able to locate and read this book is clear evidence of some degree of smarts. So ... read on!

I can also state with certainty that by the time you finish this book, you will be even smarter than you are now. Again—how can I say that? Because you will have stretched your brain responding to the questions, learned the correct answers while scoring your results, become aware of your IQ score and percentile rank, and learned some important facts about how the gift of intelligence is distributed throughout the world. That's a smart investment, one would think.

Since the tests and exercises in this book run from general to specific, you will probably benefit most from completing the first two chapters before proceeding to the later ones.

How *Not* to Use This Book

Let me begin by stating what I restate in sidebars throughout this text. The tests in this book are for personal information and entertainment only. They should *not* be used as tools for determining definite IQ or aptitude scores, academic or job placement, or learning difficulties.

Testing for such purposes requires a structured and supervised environment and includes the possible need for individual administration by a licensed psychologist.

What the tests in this book *can* provide is valuable information about your strong and weak areas, thereby helping you consider new options. Just as we say in a self-growth workshop, this book can point you in the right direction—but you must take it from there. If you see that you or someone else may need help with a difficult area, you should consult with a psychologist or a medical or educational specialist. If you appear to have a strong area, you may decide to study it further or maybe even consider a new hobby or career. Either way, people who have tried these tests report that it's usually fun taking the IQ tests and attempting the exercises in the later chapters. So go ahead ... make the most of it!

Extras

Keep on the lookout for sidebars throughout the book. These contain information that can be helpful in understanding IQ testing and many related issues. They are labeled in the following way:

def•i•ni•tion

These sidebars contain definitions of words you might not be familiar with.

Did You Know?

These boxes contain interesting facts and trivia pertaining to IQ testing.

Words to the Wise

This sidebar offers guidance and suggestions for deriving long-term benefits from IQ testing as well as test-taking tips.

Caution

These sidebars contain red flags, including reminders of what *not* to do when using the material in this book.

Acknowledgments

My profound gratitude is extended to:

My agent, Janet Rosen, at Sheree Bykofsky and Associates, for suggesting me for this project.

My acquisitions editor, Michele Wells, who guided me and encouraged me with her enthusiasm for the project, as well as all the other editorial and technical staff at Alpha Books.

My friend and colleague, Rhonda Findling, a several-times-published author who introduced me to Janet Rosen.

My mother, Anne Cirillo, who passed away in 1994 but lives on in my mind as someone who believed in me and who always placed her bet on the female, whether it be the girl jockey or the woman doctor.

My father, Carmine Cirillo, who lives happily in Las Vegas. Since my youngest days, he has always been a friend as well as an intellectual companion, answering all my questions. His brilliance even guided me through writing some of the more difficult IQ questions in this book. My father has always been loving and generous in helping me educationally, financially, and emotionally.

My friend and advisor, nationally prominent entertainment lawyer Ellis Pailet, based in New Orleans, who was always there for me with excellent advice and emotional support.

My office staff, who worked tirelessly along with me on this project.

And my friends, colleagues, clients, and extended family who shared in the excitement and joy as this book progressed from inception to completion.

Trademarks

All terms mentioned in this book that are known to be or are suspected of being trademarks or service marks have been appropriately capitalized. Alpha Books and Penguin Group (USA) Inc. cannot attest to the accuracy of this information. Use of a term in this book should not be regarded as affecting the validity of any trademark or service mark.

The Overall IQ Test

In This Chapter

- ◆ Take a complete IQ test
- ◆ Review the correct answers
- ◆ Learn your IQ score
- ◆ How does your score compare with others?

Are you a logical thinker? A numerical whiz? A verbal genius? Or are you spatially inclined? Are you looking for intellectual stimulation? Find out how smart you are with the Overall Intelligence Test. This intelligence quotient (IQ) test measures several factors of intelligence, namely logical reasoning, math skills, spatial relations skills, and verbal reasoning. Carefully read each question and select your answer. You need to select an answer for every question. Some questions are designed to be difficult, so don't expect to get every one right. Your score is based on the total number correct.

> ### Words to the Wise
>
> Before you begin any IQ, academic, or aptitude test, find out whether there's a penalty for wrong answers. If there isn't, as in this test, make sure you don't leave any answers blank. On this test, because your score is based on the total number of questions correct, you have a one in four chance of getting the right answer—even on a pure guess.

Explanations are included where appropriate. This test does not require you to have any special knowledge. People from all walks of life can take it. So go on—take the test. You're just minutes away from knowing how smart you are.

> ### Caution
>
> If English is not your native language, then your reported IQ score will probably be lower than it would be if you took an IQ test in your own language. Also note that this test may not produce a valid IQ score for those younger than 16 years of age—as some questions require sophisticated skills and educational training. For a valid assessment of persons between the ages of 3 and 15, see Chapter 9.

The Overall IQ Test

This test consists of 50 questions. There is no time limit, but most people complete it within 45 minutes. Each question has four possible answers. Circle the one that you think is correct. You may use a pen, a pencil, and scrap paper, but you may not use software (computers).

Try to do the test in one sitting. To make this possible, it's best to find a place where you'll be free from distractions for the time needed to complete the test.

Don't get help from any outside sources. Your score is meaningless if obtained by someone else.

Words to the Wise

The Overall IQ Test and other tests in this book are presented for information and entertainment purposes only. They're not a substitute for psychological, educational, or medical evaluations. If you have serious concerns about any of these matters, please consult with an appropriate professional.

Begin Test

1. The word *slovenly* is most nearly the opposite of:

   a. untidy   b. healthy   c. neat   d. friendly

2. Which word means the opposite of *lethargic?*

   a. energetic   b. sympathetic   c. egregious   d. inattentive

3. Choose the word that is most similar in meaning to *obsequious:*

   a. incorrigible b. secretive   c. intelligent d. obedient

4. *Humble* is to *arrogant* as *foolish* is to:

   a. conceited   b. wise   c. silly   d. unsure

5. *Never* is to *seldom* as *always* is to:

   a. often   b. sometimes   c. usually   d. rarely

6. Which letter comes next in this series?

   A C F J ...

   a. T   b. M   c. Q   d. O

7. Which number comes next in this series?

   3, 5, 6, 10, 9 ...

   a. 17   b. 15   c. 12   d. 13

8. Which letter comes next in this series?

   Z W S N ...

   a. L   b. E   c. H   d. J

9. Which arrow comes next in this series?

a.

b.

c.

d.

10. Which name should appear next in this series?

Jones, Smith, Smythe …

a. Johnson   b. Jonasen   c. Wright   d. Zagle

11. If you rearrange the letters GANOM you get a(n):

a. vegetable   b. animal   c. fruit   d. mineral

12. By using five letters from one of these words, you create a word that means the same as *danger:*

a. delirious   b. equilibrium   c. peculiar   d. mysterious

13. If you take three sequential letters from one of these seven-letter words, you get a word that means *likely:*

a. captain   b. disdain   c. impress   d. steward

14. If you unscramble the letters MAOPENUIM, you have the name of a(n):

a. musical instrument   b. animal   c. illness   d. body part

15. When you say that a person is *misanthropic*, you mean that person is:

a. cunning   b. cynical   c. clumsy   d. animated

16. If a car traveled 24 miles in 45 minutes, how many miles per hour was it going?

a. 50   b. 55   c. 44   d. 32

17. If 2 men could clean 4 houses in 2 days, how many days would it take 4 men to clean 16 houses?

a. 3   b. 6   c. 2   d. 4

18. Which number comes next in this series?

    4, 7, 11, 16, 22 …

    a. 27   b. 31   c. 29   d. 26

19. If you add all the even numbers from 2 to 12, you get:

    a. 42   b. 24   c. 48   d. 64

20. Kathy is 42 years old and her son, Michael, is 18. How old will Michael be when his mother is twice his age?

    a. 28   b. 21   c. 30   d. 24

21. Eileen is shorter than Amanda. Talia is shorter than Laura. If Eileen is not the shortest one, who is?

    a. Amanda   b. Talia   c. Laura   d. impossible to
                                                         tell

22. If the tenth day of the month is a Sunday, the twenty-first day of the month is a:

    a. Tuesday   b. Thursday   c. Saturday   d. Monday

23. If tibs are worse than luds and gabs are better than crods, but luds are worse than crods, which is the best of the four?

    a. tibs   b. luds   c. gabs   d. crods

24. Jane's uncle's mother could be Jane's:

    a. aunt   b. mother   c. grandmother   d. cousin

25. Four people are seated from left to right in this order: Marcia, David, Allison, and Michael. If David trades places with Michael, who then trades places with Marcia, who is now sitting to the left of Allison?

    a. Marcia   b. David   c. Michael   d. impossible to
                                                         tell

26. Which word does not belong with the others?

    a. scissors   b. knife   c. glass   d. drainpipe

27. Which one does not belong with the others?

    a. France   b. England   c. Rome   d. Switzerland

28. Which one does not belong with the others?

    a. furniture   b. fingernail   c. car   d. hat

29. Which number does not belong with the others?

    a. 17   b. 24   c. 103   d. 36,815

30. Which shape does not belong with the others?

    a.   b.

    c.   d.

31. 377421668 is the same number as:

    a. 377426168   b. 37742668   c. 377421668   d. 377412668

32. 93146 read backward is:

    a. 93146   b. 46139   c. 64319   d. 64139

33. 8641293 without one number is:

    a. 8614293   b. 864193   c. 3921468   d. 8641293

34. 937468217 read backward is:

    a. 718264739   b. 712864739   c. 712846739   d. 71284739

35. 68431759 read backward is:

    a. 95173486   b. 95718346   c. 95714386   d. 95713486

36.

is to

as

is to:

a.

b.

c.

d.

37.   – (minus)

is:

a.   b.

c.   d.

38.   +

is:

a.   b.

c.   d.

39.    – (minus)

is:

a.   b.

c.   d.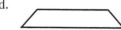

40.   – (minus)

is:

a.   b.

c.   d.

41. 3 + 14 + 17 + 28 = ?

a. 64   b. 62   c. 58   d. 54

42. 4 × 3 × 12 = ?

a. 81   b. 108   c. 154   d. 144

43. 48 – 13 + 6 – 16 = ?

a. 57   b. 65   c. 56   d. 25

44. $84 \div 2 \times 3 = ?$

    a. 246   b. 126   c. 344   d. 14

45. $14 \times 16 + 28 \div 3 = ?$

    a. 46   b. 224   c. 727   d. 84

46. How many toothpicks would it take to spell the word WAVE without bending a toothpick or using the same toothpick twice?

    a. 12   b. 13   c. 7   d. 11

47. If you move 7 feet right, 6 feet down, 2 feet left, and 3 feet up, you will be how many feet from your starting point?

    a. 12   b. 8   c. 7   d. 11

48. You are driving from Cromwell to Yurang and pass Allehen before stopping at Halloral, which is halfway to your final destination, and then you continue to Yurang. Which is the shortest distance?

    a. Cromwell to Allehen   b. Allehen to Halloral

    c. Halloral to Yurang   d. impossible to tell

49. Four gears are connected in a straight line at equal distances from one another. If the third gear is only half as big as the first gear and all the other gears are the same size, how much faster than the first gear is the fourth gear moving?

    a. twice as fast   b. four times as fast

    c. same speed   d. impossible to tell

50. If you drive north 10 miles, east 5 miles, south 7 miles, and west 3 miles, how far would you be from your starting point?

    a. 8 miles   b. 2 miles   c. 6 miles   d. 5 miles

Finish Test

Computing Your Overall IQ Score

The process of obtaining your total IQ score is easy once you have added your number of correct test responses. The answer key is located in Appendix A. Give yourself one point for each correct answer. Then, compute your total number of correct responses.

The following chart helps you determine your Overall IQ Score and where you stand in relation to the population at large.

Total IQ Scores and Percentiles

Number Correct	Percentile	IQ Score
50	99	135
49	98	130
	97	128
48	96	127
	95	125
47	94	124
	93	123
46	92	122
	91	121
45	90	120
	89	119
44	88	118
	87	117
43	86	116
	85	115
42	84	114
	83	114
41	82	114
	81	113
40	80	113
	79	112
39	78	112
	77	111
38	76	111
	75	110
37	74	110
	73	109

continues

Total IQ Scores and Percentiles (continued)

Number Correct	Percentile	IQ Score
36	72	109
	71	108
35	70	108
	69	107
34	68	107
	67	106
33	66	106
	65	106
32	64	105
	63	105
31	62	104
	61	104
30	60	104
	59	103
29	58	103
	57	102
28	56	102
	55	101
27	54	101
26	53	101
	51	100
25	50	100
	49	100
24	48	100
	47	99
23	46	99
	45	98
22	44	98
	43	97
21	42	97
	41	96

Number Correct	Percentile	IQ Score
20	40	95
	39	95
19	38	94
	37	94
18	36	94
	35	94
17	34	94
	33	94
16	32	93
	31	93
15	30	92
	29	92
14	28	91
	27	91
13	26	90
	25	90
12	24	89
	23	88
11	22	88
	21	87
10	20	87
	19	86
9	18	86
	17	85
8	16	84
	15	83
7	14	83
	13	83
6	12	82
	11	81
5	10	80
	9	79

continues

Total IQ Scores and Percentiles (continued)

Number Correct	Percentile	IQ Score
4	8	78
	7	77
3	6	76
	5	75
2	4	74
	3	73
1	2	71
0	1	70

Interpreting Your Score in Relation to Others

Let's say that you correctly answered 28 of the 50 questions on this exam. This places you at the 56th percentile with an IQ score of 102, which is in the average range. What that means is that you scored higher than 56 percent of the population while the remaining 44 percent scored higher than you. The following chart illustrates the percentage of the population that can be expected to fall within each IQ range.

Intelligence Classifications

IQ	Classification	Percent
>130	Very Superior	2.2
120–129	Superior	6.7
110–119	High Average	16.1
90–109	Average	50.0
80–89	Low Average	16.1
70–7	Borderline Deficient	6.7
<69	Deficient	2.2

Implications of Your Score

As you can observe, 50 percent of people fall within the average range (an IQ score between 90 and 109). Eighty percent of all IQ scores fall between 80 and 120. Only 10 percent fall below 75 or above 125. As we approach the extremes, we find fewer and fewer people scoring at that level. Only 1 percent of the population attains a score of 135 or higher, which is the cutoff point for genius.

Did You Know? _____

The international high-IQ society Mensa uses an IQ score of 130 or performance in the top 2 percent on a standardized test such as the Scholastic Aptitude Test (SAT) as its criterion for admitting new members.

Observe the distribution of IQ scores as displayed on the normal curve.

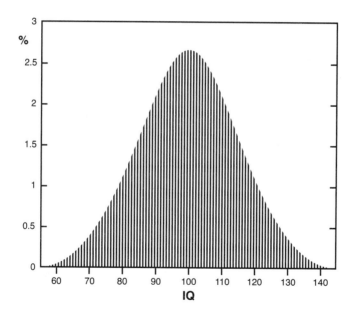

Words to the Wise

IQ and percentile *range* is used, as opposed to a number, when discussing performance on specific subtests. This is due to the fact that a small sample of questions is not a highly reliable measure of a person's skill in a particular area. Later chapters provide more in-depth measures of specific skill areas.

2

Understanding Subtest IQ Ranges

In This Chapter

◆ Calculate your subtest IQ ranges

◆ Understand the meanings behind your high and low subtest scores

◆ Discover suggestions for maximizing your strengths and improving your weaker areas

To find your score in each of the special abilities measured by The Overall IQ Test in Chapter 1, simply add the number of correct answers for that particular subtest. Do your calculations, and fill in your total number correct in the spaces beneath each subtest answer key.

When you've obtained the total number correct for each of the 10 subtests, fill in the numbers in the spaces below each corresponding subtest.

Subtest Scores and Their Meanings

	Vocabulary	Pattern Recognition	Verbal Reasoning	Mathematical Reasoning	Logic
Total Correct	___	___	___	___	___
IQ Range	___	___	___	___	___
Percentile Range	___	___	___	___	___
Classification	___	___	___	___	___

Classification	Short-Term Memory	Spatial Ability	Mathematical Computation	Visualization
Total Correct	___	___	___	___
IQ Range	___	___	___	___
Percentile Range	___	___	___	___
Classification	___	___	___	___

Use the information in the IQ range, percentile range, and classification based on your number correct for each subtest.

Subtest IQ Range, Percentile Range, and Classification

Number Correct	Classification	Subtest IQ Range	Percentile Range
5	Very Superior	130	98
4	Superior	115–129	85–98
3	High Average	100–114	50–84
2	Low Average	85–99	15–49
1	Borderline Deficient	70–84	2–14
0	Deficient	<70	<2

If you got three questions right on the spatial ability subtest, for example, your IQ level in that area would be between 100 and 114. This score places you in the average to above-average range in spatial skills and means that you scored higher than 50 to 84 percent of the general population.

Did You Know?

IQ and percentile range are used as opposed to a number when discussing performance on specific subtests. This is due to the fact that a small sample is not a very reliable measure of a person's skill in a particular area. Later chapters provide more in-depth measures of specific skill areas.

Interpreting Your Verbal Subtest Scores

The following subtests measure your verbal ability, involving such skills as word comprehension and language proficiency.

Vocabulary

This subtest measures the ability to understand the meaning of words. You must be able to perceive subtle differences among words in order to use them correctly. Consider the following question:

Which word means the opposite of *lethargic?*

a. egregious   b. sympathetic
c. vivacious   d. inattentive

Answer: c. vivacious

Persons scoring high on this vocabulary subtest tend to become writers, journalists, teachers, and lawyers. Others see these people as having "a way with words," and they often participate in activities involving debate and writing skills.

Here are some tips for improving your vocabulary:

◆ Play games such as Scrabble and word sudoku.

◆ Do crossword puzzles.

◆ Read all types of materials and look up the meaning of unknown words.

◆ Make up associations between new words and words that you already know.

Pattern Recognition

Pattern recognition is the ability to make sense of a situation by perceiving the underlying rule or logic behind it, simply stated. In other words, this skill is demonstrated when making order from chaos.

Here's an example of a pattern recognition question:

Which letter comes next in this series: Z W S N ...

a. L   b. E   c. H   d. J

Answer: c. H

People who score high on pattern recognition questions tend to appreciate the fields of art, music, and poetry. Of all subtest scores, pattern recognition correlates most highly with overall intelligence. The ability to recognize the underlying principle of organization is necessary to perform the activities required in reading, mathematics, spatial ability, logic, and classification. Pattern recognition is a skill that is largely innate and untrainable.

Verbal Reasoning

As stated previously, this subtest measures how well you can reason with words. If you performed well on this measure, you can easily find the right word in most situations. This enables you to communicate effectively by using language. Consider the following sample question:

> If you take three sequential letters from one of these seven-letter words, you get a word that means *likely:*
>
> a. impress   b. disdain   c. captain   d. steward

Answer: c. captain

People who excel in verbal reasoning often become writers, lecturers, lawyers, or teachers.

Here are some tips for improving your verbal reasoning skills:

◆ Practice writing letters, short stories, or step-by-step instructions for a project.

◆ Play out both sides of an argument in your mind, analyzing the pros and cons of each viewpoint.

◆ Read and practice reading comprehension exercises.

◆ Figure out unknown words based on their contexts.

Mathematical Reasoning

This subtest measures how well you think in numbers. Many everyday mental tasks require some numerical skills, such as figuring out how much money is needed to pay for an item or budgeting your income. Consider the following sample question:

> If a car traveled 24 miles in 45 minutes, how many miles per hour was it going?
>
> a. 50   b. 55   c. 44   d. 32

Answer: d. 32

Here are some tips to increase your mathematical reasoning skills:

◆ Calculate the tip and review the bill when you're in a restaurant.

◆ Figure out the amount of gasoline needed for the miles covered to and from a destination.

◆ Plan your budget one month ahead; consider possible unforeseen events such as medical expenses. Put "rainy day" money aside for these unpredictable occurrences.

Logic

Otherwise known as rational thinking, logic is your ability to solve a problem by following a consistent and methodical set of steps. If you scored high on this subtest, you have a strong understanding of cause and effect relationships and can thereby predict the likely consequences of certain actions. Here is a sample logic question:

Jane's uncle's mother could be Jane's:

a. aunt   b. mother   c. grandmother   d. cousin

Answer: c. grandmother

People who have strong logic skills often do well in jobs involving developing arguments, such as law or grant writing. If combined with a high mathematical reasoning score, these people often become design engineers or computer program developers.

Here are some tips for increasing your logic skills:

◆ Play a game such as chess, which involves planning and strategy.

◆ Solve word problems and practice logic puzzles.

◆ Work puzzles, such as connecting dots and brain teasers.

Classification

This subtest measures the ability to note similarities among objects and then place them into the appropriate categories.

Here's an example of a classification question:

> Which number does not belong with the others?
>
> a. 17   b. 24   c. 103   d. 36,815

Answer: b. 24 (all the others are odd numbers)

People who score high in classification perform well on tasks requiring discrimination and conceptual understanding of the relationships between objects. They are often scientists, laboratory technicians, librarians, or clerical workers. These skills can also help you memorize information and adapt to new situations. Because classification relies heavily on other skills such as visualization, memory, and logic, the best activities to practice for improving your classification skills are those associated with logic, visualization, and memory.

Short-Term Memory

This subtest is a measure of your ability to learn information and retain it for a limited amount of time. Short-term memory is also a strong measure of attention and concentration.

Here's a sample short-term memory subtest question:

> 68431759 read backward is:
>
> a. 95173486
>
> b. 95718346
>
> c. 95714386
>
> d. 95713486

Answer: d. 95713486

People who have a strong short-term memory do well at activities requiring quick adaptation to new situations and the ability to "think on your feet." Jobs that require speaking, such as sales and reporting, or police and detective work, may be well suited for you if you did well on the short-term memory subtest.

Here are some tips for improving your short-term memory:

◆ "Chunk" information into smaller bits (for example, 4 1 6 7 4 3 5 2 9 7 is easier to remember when it becomes 416-743-5297).

◆ Say items out loud.

◆ Use *mnemonic* devices to give meaning to unrelated bits of information.

def•i•ni•tion

> **Mnemonics** are memory-enhancing strategies that involve linking information that you already know to new information. An example would be combining the first letters of each word in a sentence to spell one easily recognized word or sound, such as MADD to refer to Mothers Against Drunk Driving.

Interpreting Your Nonverbal Subtest Scores

The following subtests measure your nonverbal abilities, involving such skills as math and visualization.

Spatial Ability

Simply stated, spatial ability is the capacity to visualize objects in space. If you score high on this subtest, you can manipulate and rotate objects in your mind and easily picture the outcome.

Spatial ability is an excellent measure of raw intelligence without prior training or knowledge.

Here is a sample spatial ability question:

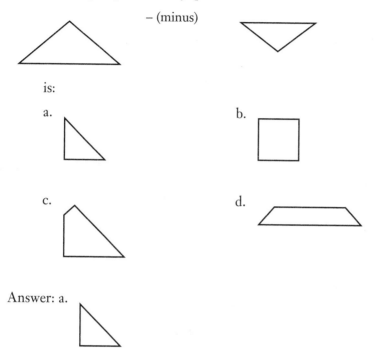

People who have strong spatial ability tend to perform well on tasks that require thinking in terms of images and manipulating objects. They often gravitate toward fields such as architecture, engineering, design, and aviation. (After all, an airline pilot needs a good sense of direction!)

Here are some tips for improving spatial ability:

- ◆ Read maps and plan directions for anticipated trips.

- ◆ Pack boxes, groceries, and suitcases to ensure the best possible fit.

- ◆ Play with Legos, building blocks, puzzles, and mazes.

Mathematical Computation

The ability to add, subtract, multiply, and divide numbers mentally leads to high performance on this subtest. This test measures your ability to perform basic arithmetic calculations.

Here's a sample mathematical computation question:

48 - 13 + 6 - 16 = ?

a. 57   b. 65   c. 56   d. 25

Answer: d. 25

People who score high on the mathematical computation subtest perform well as accountants, scientists, and stockbrokers.

Here are some tips for improving your mathematical computation skills:

- Balance your checkbook without using a calculator. You can verify the results later.

- Use a pen and paper to perform calculations.

- Do multiplication flash cards in your head until you have completely memorized the "times tables."

Visualization

Visualization is the ability to think and communicate with pictures. A person who has a high score on the visualization subtest can perceive visual patterns and extract that information for further use.

Here's a sample visualization question:

If you drive north 10 miles, east 5 miles, south 7 miles, and west 3 miles, how far would you be from your starting point?

a. 8 miles   b. 2 miles   c. 6 miles   d. 5 miles

Answer: d. 5 miles

People who have strong visualization skills often become artists, designers, decorators, and cosmetic surgeons.

Here are some tips for improving your visualization ability:

- Sketch and draw objects.

- Picture images that go along with words you hear.

◆ Play board and computer games involving visual coordination and calculations.

◆ Form associations between words and pictures, and test your memory at a later time.

> **Caution**
>
> Nonverbal subtests are more affected by emotional states (nervousness, anger, depression, and so on) than verbal subtests are. If you scored much lower on all nonverbal subtests, a retake when you are in a better state of mind may be in order.

High and Low Areas: What Do They Mean?

Your performance on specialized tasks or academic tests measuring specific skills can be equal to, greater than, or less than your general ability.

Subtest Scores Versus Overall Test Score

Let's say that you obtained an overall IQ score of 110. This score is in the high average range and places you at the 90th percentile of the population with regard to general intelligence. Now, what if you obtained that high average score despite the fact that your spatial ability score was in the low average range? At least one, if not more, of your other subtests had to be higher than the high average range to prevent the overall score from being dragged downward. We can safely say that you, like me (see the following sidebar), have a significant weakness in spatial ability skills.

Understanding Your Intellectual Strengths

Suppose you scored high in logic, visualization, and numerical reasoning. You'd probably be well suited for activities that employ a combination of these skills, such as computer-aided design and engineering. You probably also enjoy these activities and may be headed down this (or a similar) vocational path. Why? The answer is simple. We keep doing the things we're good at because they're easy—and success feels good. Therefore, we get more and more practice at these activities, so we get better and better at performing them. If you are good in math, people hand you the restaurant check to scan for errors and figure out the tip. If you're mechanical, you tend to jump in first and set up equipment. This, of course, leads to our next topic of discussion.

> **Words to the Wise** _____
>
> It's all relative. The same subtest IQ range may be a strength for one person and a weakness for another, depending on how it compares with the overall IQ test score.

Understanding Your Intellectual Weaknesses

So what about those subtests that were significantly lower in IQ range than your overall IQ score? I'll bet you avoid these activities whenever possible. Why? Because the awkward steps of an unfamiliar task, along with struggle and failure, feels bad. So while we continue to practice the activities in which we are talented—thereby getting better and better at performance—we avoid those activities that don't come naturally and involve more struggle to perform. Therefore, we get little or no practice in those difficult areas—so there are fewer opportunities to improve our performance.

The cycle runs as follows:

Good performance—practice—better performance

Bad performance—no practice—no improvement

> **Words to the Wise** _____
>
> If you scored low on a particular subtest, refer to the subtest explanations in this chapter and try practicing the self-improvement activities suggested under that particular subtest. Retake the test or a similar test in three months and see whether your score shows any improvement.

Tips for Improving Your Score

Learn how to make the most of what you do best.

Maximize Your Strengths

◆ Become involved in extracurricular activities and hobbies that involve your areas of ability.

◆ Get to know others who are similarly skilled, and exchange ideas.

◆ Refine your skills by taking lessons or participating in difficult exercises that will bring you to the next level.

Minimize and Improve Your Weak Areas

◆ Take lessons where needed. People who have natural athletic ability may be able to learn a sport by simply jumping in and doing it. Others may need more guidance and step-by-step instructions, however.

◆ While you need to learn from the masters, it often helps to obtain pointers from those who have also struggled to learn the same skills. Why? They sometimes know the pitfalls better than the masters (to whom the skills come naturally). This leads to my next suggestion.

◆ Teach. That's right. Studies have shown that children (and adults) who are poor at reading are better at teaching reading than those who are good at reading and may automatically leave out a few steps.

Words to the Wise

I've received compliments for giving good directions. Because I'm aware of the pitfalls, I leave nothing to the imagination. Knowing where I'm likely to become confused (for example, "This is a very sharp turn that comes up immediately after the light"), I can warn the other person to avoid mistakes.

Implications of Your Score

It's important to remember that:

◆ Everyone has intellectual strengths and weaknesses.

◆ You can determine your high-ability and low-ability areas through detailed analysis of IQ test results.

◆ There are things you can do to improve performance in both strong and weak intellectual skills.

3

Culture-Fair IQ Tests

In This Chapter

◆ Define "culture-fair" tests

◆ Test your IQ with several culture-fair instruments

◆ Score and interpret your test results

◆ Compare these results with prior scores on other measures

What is a culture-fair IQ test? Simply stated, it's a test that's designed to measure intelligence while minimizing cultural or educational bias. The IQ tests in this chapter are based on image patterns, letters, and numbers that test the ability to learn and use new information without any prior knowledge needed.

You May Be Smarter than You Think!

Intelligence tests often report two kinds of scores: verbal and nonverbal. The nonverbal score is determined by having an individual perform a variety of activities involving pattern recognition, mathematical reasoning, and spatial skills that don't involve language. The culture-fair IQ tests in this chapter rely mainly on nonverbal skills. If you have a history of difficulty with language or academic skills, the tests in this chapter may provide a better estimate of your real intellectual potential.

> **Caution**
>
> Because of the nature of the activities, culture-fair tests (and most nonverbal tasks) rely heavily on visual ability. Make certain the lighting is good, and if you need any visual aids (reading glasses, contact lenses, and so on), be sure to use them.

Take These Culture-Fair Tests

The following tests measure specific intellectual skills, without relying upon education or formalized training or knowledge.

Paired-Item Memory IQ Test

This test consists of 10 pairs of items. Allow yourself two minutes to memorize them. Use a stopwatch or other timing device to ensure that the timing is exact. You may study the items, but do not write any of them on paper or use any software. After studying the items for two minutes, begin the quiz. Do not refer back to the items while taking the quiz, and do not obtain help from anyone else. You may use scrap paper while working on the quiz items.

Here are the paired items. Begin timing:

1. 9 6 B Z = $ J A
2. 2 8 $ 2 = T 1 6
3. 6 4 D ! = A B Z
4. 8 7 T A = 2 2 C
5. 4 8 1 X = $! ? 2
6. 8 6 1 W = 2 H K C
7. 9 5 ! ? = $ 2 1 6

8. 8 8 2 1 4 = 9 4 A

9. 9 6 8 D T = Z Z Y W 6

10. 8 1 T 4 6 = A B E 7 6

Now cover up the paired items above and take the following quiz. There is no time limit.

Begin Quiz
---

1. 2 8 $ 2 =

    a. A B Z

    b. $! ? 2

    c. 2 H K C

    d. T 1 6

2. 4 8 1 X =

    a. $! ? 2

    b. Z Z Y W 6

    c. 9 4 A

    d. A B E 7 6

3. 8 6 1 W =

    a. $ 2 1 6

    b. 2 H K C

    c. Z Z Y W 6

    d. A B E 7 6

4. 8 1 T 4 6 =

    a. $ 2 1 6

    b. 2 2 C

    c. A B E 7 6

    d. 9 4 A

5. 9 6 B Z =

    a. T 1 6

    b. $ J A

    c. A B E 7 6

    d. 9 4 A

6. 9 6 8 D T =

    a. Z Z Y W 6

    b. T 1 6

    c. $ 2 1 6

    d. 2 2 C

7. 9 5 ! ? =

    a. A B E 7 6

    b. $ 2 1 6

    c. A B Z

    d. 9 4 A

8. 8 7 T A =

    a. Z Z Y W 6

    b. 2 2 C

    c. T 1 6

    d. 2 H K C

9. 6 4 D 1 =

    a. T 1 6

    b. 2 H K C

    c. A B Z

    d. $! ? 2

10. 8 8 2 1 4 =

    a. $! ? 2

    b. A B E 7 6

    c. Z Z Y W 6

    d. 9 4 A

End Quiz

See Appendix A for answers.

Score_____

The following chart will help you determine your memory IQ range and where you stand in relation to others.

Paired-Item Memory IQ Test—Results and Interpretation

Number Correct	IQ Range	Classification	Percentile
9–10	140	Very Superior	99.9
7–8	130–139	Very Superior	98–99.8
5–6	120–129	Superior	90–97
4	110–119	High Average	75–89
3	100–109	Average	50–74
2	90–99	Average	25–49
0–1	<90	Below Average	<25

If you got 9 or 10 correct on this difficult memory task, you are a genius. (Either that or you cheated and looked at the items, in which case your score is invalid.) Assuming you followed the instructions honestly, even 2 to 3 out of 10 correct places you in the average range (an IQ between 90 and 109).

Nonverbal Abstract Reasoning IQ Test

Examine these items and choose the option that best replaces the question mark. The symbol ":" means "is to." For example:

    a : (is to) b as c : (is to)?

There is no time limit for this test.

Begin Test

1. :  as : ?

   a.   b.

   c.   d.

2. : as : ?

   a.   b.

   c.   d.

3. : as  : ?

a.

b.

c.

d.

4. : as : ?

a.

b.

c.

d.

5.   :   as   : ?

a.

b.

c.

d.

For the following images, choose the best option to replace the question mark.

6.

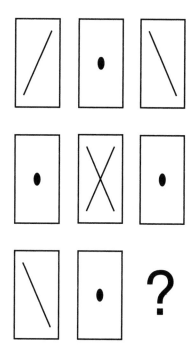

a.

b.

c.

d.

7.

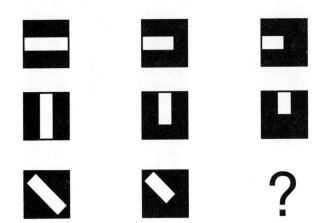

a.

b.

c.

d.

8.

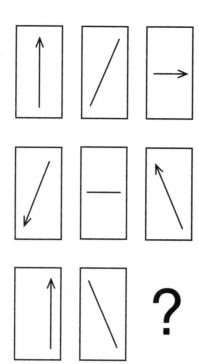

a.

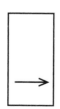

b.

c.

d.

9.

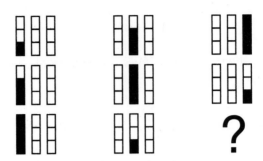

a.

b.

c.

d.

10.

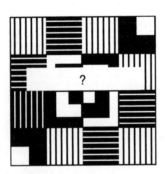

a.

b.

c.

d.

See Appendix A for answers.

Score_____

The following chart will help you determine your nonverbal abstract reasoning IQ range.

Nonverbal Abstract Reasoning IQ Test—Results and Interpretation

Number Correct	IQ Range	Classification	Percentile
9–10	130	Very Superior	98
7–8	115–129	Superior	85–98
5–6	100–114	High Average	50–84
3–4	85–99	Low Average	15–49
1–2	70–84	Borderline Deficient	2–14
0	<70	Deficient	<2

Most people score within the middle range. If you got 3 out of 10 correct, your score is in the low average range (with an IQ score between 85 and 99 in nonverbal abstract reasoning). This result would place you higher than 15 to 49 percent of the population.

Pattern Recognition IQ Test

Now try the following test. There is no time limit.

Begin Test

Which comes next in the following series?

1. 1, 2, 4, 7, 11 ...

    a. 16   b. 25   c. 36   d. 18

2. 4, 9, 16, 25, 36 ...

    a. 45   b. 49   c. 64   d. 52

3. 64, 63, 61, 58 ...

    a. 55   b. 53   c. 54   d. 56

4. 3, 7, 15, 31, 63 …

   a. 127   b. 112   c. 78   d. 247

5. 1, 8, 27, 64, 125 …

   a. 345   b. 256   c. 428   d. 216

6. U S Q O …

   a. V   b. P   c. N   d. M

7. 22D 68N 51F 92K 36?

   a. I   b. H   c. G   d. K

8. 23F 43L 21B 38X 29?

   a. G   b. R   c. U   d. H

End Test

See Appendix A for answers.

Score_____

Use the following chart to determine your pattern recognition IQ—range, percentile, and classification.

Pattern Recognition IQ Test—Results and Interpretation

Number Correct	IQ Range	Classification	Percentile
9–10	130	Very Superior	98
7–8	115–129	Superior	85–98
5–6	100–114	High average	50–84
3–4	85–99	Low Average	15–49
1–2	70–84	Borderline Deficient	2–14
0	<70	Deficient	<2

If you answered 5 out of 10 questions correctly, this would place you in the high average range on this measure with an IQ score between 100 and 114, which is between the 50th and 84th percentile of the general population.

Mazes IQ Test

You have exactly 15 minutes to complete the following five mazes. Use a stopwatch or other appropriate timing device to ensure that your timing is exact. Make sure that you work steadily without distractions. Do not obtain help from anyone else. Begin each maze at point B, and end each maze at point E.

Caution

Because the Mazes IQ Test is timed and relies heavily on fine visual-motor coordination, people who have any type of disability in this area should not use it as a valid instrument to obtain an IQ range. You may use this test for fun and practice instead.

Begin Test

1. Maze Number 1

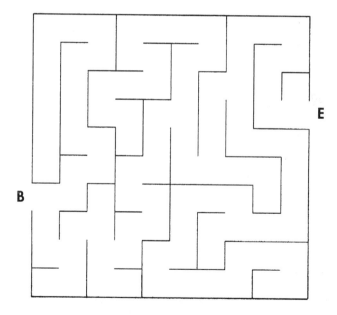

2. Maze Number 2

B

E

3. Maze Number 3

B

E

4. Maze Number 4

B

E

5. Maze Number 5

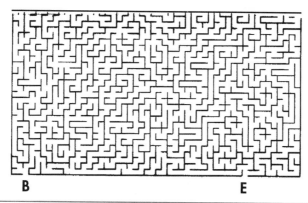

B   E

End Test

See Appendix A for maze solutions.

Score_____

The following chart will help you determine your Mazes IQ range and standing in relation to others.

Mazes IQ Test—Results and Interpretation

Number Correct	IQ Range	Classification	Percentile
5	130	Very Superior	98
4	115–129	Superior	85–98
3	100–114	High Average	50–84
2	85–99	Low Average	15–49
1	70–84	Borderline Deficient	2–14
0	<70	Deficient	<2

Let's say you finished 4 out of 5 mazes correctly within the 15-minute time limit. This means you scored higher than 85 to 98 percent of the population with a Mazes IQ range of 115 to 129, which places you in the superior category.

Did You Know?

Rats, mice, and other animals demonstrate great variability in IQ levels. Mazes are the most common test used to assess rats' intelligence levels.

Implications of Your Score

Now that you've had the chance to measure your success on several IQ tests that don't rely upon prior knowledge or education, you can compare these results with your past history. If you note a significant difference (more than 15 points) between your scores on the tests in this chapter and other more language-dependent and verbal tests, it may be helpful to review language or other academic subjects. Once again, you may be smarter than you think.

4

General Aptitude Tests

In This Chapter

◆ Test your performance in specific academic areas

◆ Test your skills in nonacademic areas

◆ Score and interpret your results

◆ Become aware of your best and worst academic and nonacademic abilities

Human beings are gifted with a certain amount of innate potential, otherwise known as intelligence. This determines the upper limit of your capacity to learn. Within this limit, there is a *vast* amount of room for developing and refining special academic and work-related skills. While ability is *innate*, aptitude is *learned*. This chapter explores the extent and type of learning that you've acquired over the course of your lifetime.

Language Arts Test

The following test contains questions that determine how skillful you are in using the English language. Answer each question by circling the best response.

> **Caution** ———————————————————————
> This is not a valid IQ measure for you if English is not your native language. If this is the case, use the questions for fun and practice only.

Begin Test

1. What is the name for a word that signifies a person, place, or thing?

    a. noun   b. verb   c. adjective   d. adverb

2. What is the name for a word that is used in a sentence to denote action?

    a. noun   b. verb   c. adjective   d. adverb

3. Choose the adjective in this sentence:

    The girl carried a white bag.

    a. girl   b. carried   c. white   d. bag

4. Choose the verb from the above sentence.

    a. girl   b. carried   c. white   d. bag

5. Choose the adverb from this sentence:

    He finished the job surprisingly fast.

    a. he   b. finished   c. surprisingly   d. fast

6. _____ are words that sound alike but are spelled differently and have different meanings.

    a. acronyms   b. synonyms   c. antonyms   d. homonyms

7. LOL is a(n):

    a. acronym   b. synonym   c. antonym   d. homonym

Select the correct spelling for the following words:

8. a. polyphony   b. polyfonies   c. polyfonie   d. polyphonie

9. a. vengance   b. vengince   c. vengience   d. vengeance

10. a. theripeutic   b. thereputic   c. theraputic   d. therapeutic

11. a. gastrnomie   b. gastronomy   c. gastranomy   d. gastranomie

12. a. solidarity   b. solitarity   c. solidarrity   d. solitarie

13. a. transitional   b. transitonal   c. transittional   d. transentional

14. a. harminize   b. harmoniz   c. harrminze   d. harmonize

15. a. sliedgehamer   b. sledgehammer
    c. sledghammer   d. slegehammer

16. a. decelerate   b. decellerate   c. decelerait   d. deceliarate

17. a. giomerule   b. glomberule   c. glomeraule   d. glomerule

18. a. entrakrainial   b. entrancranial   c. intracranial   d. intrachranial

19. a. dyosees   b. diosese   c. digsese   d. diocese

20. a. yoakel   b. yokel   c. yokelie   d. yohkei

Complete the following sentences:

21. Put your money where your _____ is.

    a. foot   b. mouth   c. head   d. nose

22. Be careful what you wish for …

    a. it might not come true

    b. it might come true

    c. it might not be what you want

    d. it might be too much to handle

23. Money doesn't grow on …

    a. paper   b. banks   c. branches   d. trees

24. Break a(n) …

    a. arm   b. head   c. leg   d. nose

25. I brought you into this world …

    a. I can send you back

    b. I can't take you out

    c. I can take you out

    d. I can bring you up

What do the following expressions mean?

26. Genius is 1 percent inspiration and 99 percent perspiration.

    a. The genius is in the top 1 percent.

    b. Geniuses are smarter than 99 percent of people everywhere.

    c. He or she who sweats the most does best.

    d. The idea is innate, but it's what you do with it that makes it genius.

27. The die is cast.

    a. I placed my bet down.

    b. There's no turning back.

    c. The money changed hands.

    d. None of the above.

28. To "get one's goat":

    a. annoy someone

    b. steal property

    c. get satisfaction

    d. fool someone

29. The stadium was filled with yellow bees.

    a. There was a bee's nest above the stadium.

    b. The crowd was heavily weighed to one team.

    c. Everyone wore yellow uniforms.

    d. The crowd was noisy and buzzing.

30. Elvis has left the building!

    a. The fight has ended.

    b. The show is over.

    c. Elvis is dead.

    d. Elvis is hiding out somewhere.

For the answers, see Appendix A.

The following chart will show you where you stand in relation to others in language arts.

Language Arts Test–Results and Interpretation

Number Correct	IQ Range	Classification	Percentile
27–30	130	Very Superior	98
23–26	115–129	Superior	85–98
19–22	100–114	High Average	50–84
15–19	85–99	Low Average	15–49
8–14	70–84	Borderline Deficient	2–14
<8	<70	Deficient	<2

If you got 19 right, you scored in the average range. This means that your performance on academic and work-related tasks requiring verbal abstract reasoning (the ability to recognize the meaning of common expressions), grammar, and spelling is at about the same level as most people.

Mathematical Achievement Test

How well do you reason with numbers? Let's find out.

Begin Test

1. If 2 coins add up to 30 cents and the first coin is not a nickel, what are the 2 coins?

   a. dime and quarter

   b. quarter and nickel

   c. nickel and quarter

   d. quarter and dime

2. What is $6 + 6 + 6 - 6 - 6 - 6$?

   a. 666   b. 666,666   c. 36   d. 0

3. Susan is twice as old as her sister and half as old as her mother. Her sister is 12 years old. How old is her mother?

   a. 28   b. 24   c. 48   d. 36

4. Talia is both the 50th best student in the class and the 50th worst student. How many students are in the class?

   a. 99   b. 101   c. 100   d. 51

5. Which number comes next in this series:

   14, 24, 68, 38, 45 ...

   a. 15   b. 73   c. 86   d. 98

6. Which number does not belong with the others?

   a. 38   b. 27   c. 7   d. 4

7. There were 10 people at a meeting. They shook hands at the beginning and end of the meeting. How many handshakes were there?

   a. 20   b. 40   c. 86   d. 106

8. You have a box filled with six red marbles, four black ones, and eight blue ones. What percent chance is there of picking a black one?

   a. 10%   b. 18%   c. 25%   d. 50%

End Test

> **Words to the Wise**
>
> If you don't use it, you lose it. While all scores in academic areas diminish without use or refresher courses, mathematical skills are particularly vulnerable to this type of erosion. One explanation for this fact is that while language skills are used in everyday living, those involving mathematics are more specialized and therefore not practiced, so they are more easily forgotten.

For the answers, see Appendix A.

The following chart will show you where you stand in relation to others in terms of mathematical achievement.

Mathematical Achievement Test–Results and Interpretation

Number Correct	IQ Range	Classification	Percentile
8	130	Very Superior	98
6–7	115–129	Superior	85–98
5	10–114	High Average	50–84
3–4	85–99	Low Average	15–49
2	70–84	Borderline Deficient	2–14
0–1	<70	Deficient	<2

Did You Know?

What doesn't kill you raises your IQ. Numerous studies show that a person's IQ score can be 10 to 20 points higher one to two years after going through a highly stressful life event, e.g., divorce, loss of a loved one, job loss, or unwanted move. This has been observed in persons of all ages. However, before we prescribe stress as a method of intellectual stimulation, we must also note that higher rates of death and illness also coincide with stressful events.

Acuity Skills Test

The following test measures how quickly you can perform certain activities. You have three minutes to complete the questions. Timing must be exact, so use a stopwatch or other timepiece. You may use scrap paper and pencil but no software. Work alone in an undisturbed environment and work as quickly as possible.

Begin Test

1. $16 + 8 =$

   a. 24   b. 36   c. 8   d. 26

2. $23 + 48 =$

   a. 83   b. 71   c. 25   d. 27

3. $9 \times 12 =$

   a. 98   b. 144   c. 112   d. 108

4. $876 - 28 =$

   a. 742   b. 862   c. 268   d. 848

5. $32 + 684 + 26 =$

   a. 742   b. 862   c. 268   d. 192

6. $84 \times 6 =$

   a. 484   b. 504   c. 78   d. 90

7. $4,085 - 279 =$

   a. 3,864   b. 3,966   c. 3,806   d. 6,789

8. $49 \times 7 =$

   a. 343   b. 497   c. 42   d. 56

9. $568 - 294 =$

   a. 286   b. 274   c. 386   d. 48

10. $42 \div 6 =$

   a. 48   b. 34   c. 36   d. 7

11. $984 \div 3 =$

   a. 364   b. 328   c. 238   d. 342

12. $563 \times 96 =$

   a. 54,084   b. 54,048   c. 56,026   d. 56,260

In the following questions, select the one that should occur first alphabetically:

13. a. action   b. aardvark   c. aaa   d. aa

14. a. BBC   b. baac   c. bad   d. beck

15. a. zyth   b. zzz   c. z   d. zack

16. a. pat   b. pick   c. paaltzad   d. pal

17. a. take   b. talk   c. teacher   d. tut

18. a. xyz   b. xzc   c. xxx   d. xxxr

19. a. Alison   b. Alita   c. Alena   d. Allena

20. a. umbrella   b. uug   c. uxck   d. uuuu

End Test

For the answers, see Appendix A.

The following chart shows where you stand in relation to the general population in acuity skills.

Acuity Skills Test—Results and Interpretation

Number Correct	IQ Range	Classification	Percentile
18–20	140	Very Superior	99.9
15–17	130–139	Very Superior	98–99.8
12–14	120–129	Superior	90–97
11–13	110–119	High Average	75–89
8–10	100–109	Average	50–74
5–7	90–99	Average	25–49
<5	<90	Below Average	<25

Acuity is the ability to perform routine tasks quickly and accurately. Given equal skill and accuracy, the person who can perform a task faster is often the better one for the job. If you scored high on the Acuity Skills Test, chances are good that you would do well at jobs requiring attention and concentration and advanced math and language skills.

Spatial Skills Test

How well do you visualize objects in space?

1. What does the following figure look like when folded?

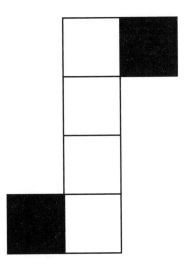

a.

b.

c.
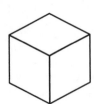

d.

2.   – (minus)   =

   a.

                               b.

   c.

                               d.

3.

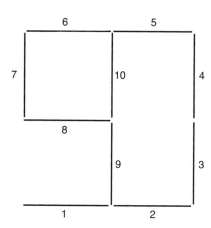

Which toothpick would you need to move in order to create two—
and only two—*squares?*

a. 8   b. 5   c. 9   d. 7

4. +  =

a.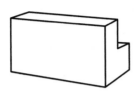

b.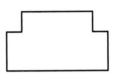

c.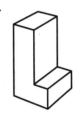

d.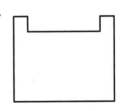

5. Which of the following figures looks the same as the preceding figure when folded?

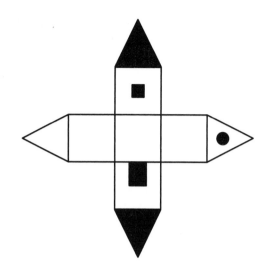

a.

b.

c.

d.

6. Which of the following figures looks the same as the preceding figure when folded?

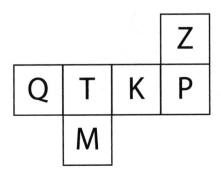

a.

b.

c.

d.

7. Which of the following figures looks the same as the preceding figure when folded?

a.

b.

c.

d.

8. If I'm traveling north and turn right 90 degrees, left 90 degrees, and then right 90 degrees, in which direction am I facing?

   a. north   b. south   c. east   d. west

9. A 4-inch cube has red paint on all six sides. It is cut into 1-inch cubes. How many 1-inch cubes will have three red sides?

   a. 8   b. 16   c. 24   d. 4

End Test

For the answers, see Appendix A.

The following chart will help you determine your spatial skills ability level.

Spatial Skills Test—Results and Interpretation

Number Correct	IQ Range	Classification	Percentile
9–10	130	Very Superior	98
7–8	115–129	Superior	85–98
5–6	100–114	High Average	50–84
3–4	85–99	Low Average	15–49
1–2	70–84	Borderline	2–14
0	<70	Deficient	<2

Mechanical Skills Test

Are you skilled mechanically? Take the following test and find out.

Begin Test

1. Find the weight to balance the scale:

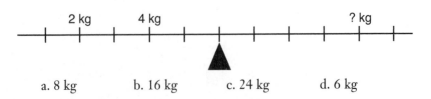

   a. 8 kg   b. 16 kg   c. 24 kg   d. 6 kg

2. If all these blocks are made of the same material, which would be the heaviest?

a.

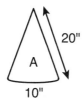

b.

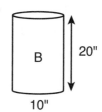

c.

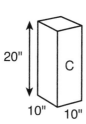

d. all are equal

3. Which pipe would hold the most water?

a. all are equal

b.

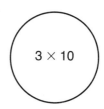

c.

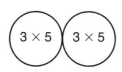

d.

4. Find the weight to balance the scale:

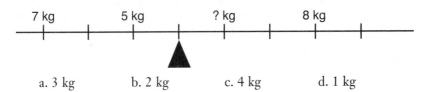

    a. 3 kg   b. 2 kg   c. 4 kg   d. 1 kg

5. If these three containers are of equal weight, made of the same material, and have equal volume capacity, which one would cool water fastest?

   a.   b.

   c.   d. all are the same

6. There are four gears connected in a row at equal distances. The first gear is twice the size of the fourth gear. How much faster would the fourth gear go than the first gear?

   a. same speed

   b. half as fast

   c. twice as fast

   d. four times as fast

7. There is a sink with three different faucets. With the smallest tap, the sink is filled in 10 minutes. With the next size tap, it's filled in 5 minutes; and with the largest tap, it's filled in 2 minutes. How long will it take for all three to fill the sink?

   a. 1 minute, 20 seconds

   b. 1 minute, 40 seconds

   c. 2 minutes

   d. 3 minutes

8. You hear a creaking sound coming from your car. What do you do?

   a. Stop and call your mechanic.

   b. Lubricate all parts, hoping to hit the right one.

   c. Ignore it. The noise will either get worse and then you'll have it serviced, or it will *hopefully* go away.

   d. Turn up your radio.

End Test

For the answers, see Appendix A.

The following chart shows where you stand in relation to others in mechanical ability.

Mechanical Skills Test—Results and Interpretation

Number Correct	IQ Range	Classification	Percentile
8	130	Very Superior	98
6–7	115–129	Superior	85–98
5	100–114	High Average	50–84
3–4	85–99	Low Average	15–49
2	70–84	Borderline Deficient	2–14
0–1	<70	Deficient	<2

Visual-Motor Speed Test

The following is a test of visualization and *fine motor skills*. Each number has a corresponding letter in the box beneath. The numbers in the next five rows do not have letters beneath them. You have two minutes to place the numbers in the boxes. Timing must be exact, so use a stopwatch or another appropriate timing device. Work as quickly as you can.

def•i•ni•tion

Fine motor skills are purposeful movements that involve small tasks such as writing, tying laces, and making crafts.

Caution

This test relies heavily on good visualization and adequate motor skills. Be sure to use any required visual aids. If you have any type of visual-motor difficulty, you should use this test for fun and practice but not as a valid aptitude measure.

Begin Test

1	2	3	4	5	6	7	8	9	10
X	C	M	J	E	A	B	T	Z	Q

4	6	1	3	9	4	7	8	6	0	3	1	5	6	2	9	1	0	4	2
3	8	0	4	6	2	1	7	5	8	6	4	2	8	1	6	9	5	1	3
8	6	4	1	6	9	0	5	3	2	7	8	0	9	4	6	3	5	0	6
6	5	2	9	5	7	1	6	4	8	9	2	1	7	8	3	2	4	1	9
1	9	8	7	3	4	2	0	6	1	2	8	5	0	6	7	1	2	9	8

End Test

For the answers, see Appendix A.

The following chart will help you determine your visual-motor aptitude.

Visual-Motor Speed Test—Results and Interpretation

Number Correct	IQ Range	Classification	Percentile
90–100	140+	Genius	99.9+
70–89	130–13	Very Superior	98–99
50–69	120–129	Superior	90–97
40–49	110–119	High Average	75–89
30–39	100–109	Average	50–74
20–29	90–99	Low Average	25–49
0–19	<90	Borderline Deficient	<25

Chapter 5

Assess Your Creativity

In This Chapter

◆ Become aware of the different functions of your right and left brain

◆ Learn which side of your brain is dominant

◆ Test your creativity

◆ Learn to maximize your total brain power

Your brain is made up of two hemispheres: the left and the right. Each side has separate functions, although some of these abilities are shared. The *corpus callosum* allows communication between the two halves.

def•i•ni•tion

The **corpus callosum** is a thick band of nerve fibers that connects the two hemispheres of the brain.

The left hemisphere specializes in logical and analytical thought, planning, general knowledge, and academic-type tasks. It also controls the right side of the body. The right hemisphere controls the *left* hand as well as the entire left side of the body. This hemisphere is responsible for visualizing, intuition, emotions, motor skills, and spatial awareness.

One side of your brain begins to dominate at the age of 2, and the process is complete by age 15.

The Brain Type Test

The following questions will help determine which half of your brain is dominant. There is no time limit, but most people complete this test within 20 minutes.

For each question, circle the alternative that most clearly describes you, your behavior, or preferences. If the statement is clearly true about you, circle *a* (strongly agree). If the statement describes you some or most of the time, circle *b* (agree). If the statement rarely describes you, circle *c* (disagree). If the statement is clearly untrue about you, circle *d* (strongly disagree).

Begin Test

1. When I have questions, I prefer to ask someone rather than do the research myself.

    a   b   c   d

2. If I ever had total amnesia, I would still remember the face of my loved one.

    a   b   c   d

3. I prefer geometry to algebra.

    a   b   c   d

4. My friends can call me anytime, day or night.

    a   b   c   d

5. My feelings ultimately determine my choices and behavior.

    a   b   c   d

6. I am easily distracted.

    a   b   c   d

7. I like being among large groups of people.

    a   b   c   d

8. I prefer reading maps to verbal directions.

    a   b   c   d

9. I often do things on the spur of the moment.

    a   b   c   d

10. I often begin many tasks at the same time.

    a   b   c   d

11. My hardest battles are with myself.

    a   b   c   d

12. I've been described as a planner and an organizer.

    a   b   c   d

13. If I have time to kill, I use it productively.

    a   b   c   d

14. I prefer to be with one person as opposed to a group.

    a   b   c   d

15. I was/am an above-average student in academic subjects.

    a   b   c   d

16. When I'm facing a decision, I first make a list of the pros and cons.

    a   b   c   d

17. I prefer structured tasks to those that are more open-ended.

    a   b   c   d

18. People describe me as independent.

    a   b   c   d

19. I have a better memory for facts and words than for faces and pictures.

    a   b   c   d

20. I don't mind working alone.

    a   b   c   d

End Test

See Appendix A for scoring directions.

The following chart describes the meaning of your score on the Brain Type Test.

Brain Type Test Results and Interpretation

Score	Percent of Population in This Category	Meaning	Suggestions
70–80	2.2	*Extreme* left brain dominance	Lighten up. Relax. Have fun and you'll be *more* successful.
59–69	6.7	Left brain *dominance*	Loosen up and experiment more.
47–58	16.1	Left brain *preference*	You're responsible.
34–46	50.0	Brain synergy	Congratulations—you are well-balanced.
22–33	16.1	Right brain *preference*	You're creative.

Score	Percent of Population in This Category	Meaning	Suggestions
11–21	6.7	Right brain *dominance*	Set goals and stay on track. Your mind tends to wander.
0–10	2.2	*Extreme* right brain dominance	You need to become a a bit more focused on the practical. Fantasy is great, but there's a whole world out there.

Look closely at the distribution of scores for the Brain Type Test. What do you see?

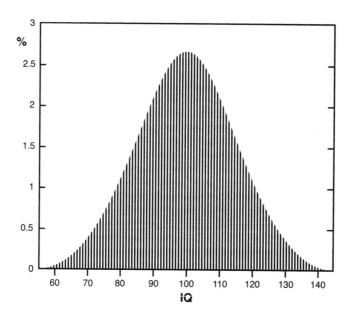

The Brain Type Test scores fall along the bell curve, with most people scoring in the middle. This is the case with most tests of intellect and ability. Extreme high and low scores are quite rare.

What's different about the Brain Type Test from previous measures we have explored is that you are not aiming for a high end but for the middle.

That's right. *Synergy* and *balance* are what you should strive for.

Did You Know? _____

Studies show that when there is injury to one side of the brain, the other side develops significantly—sometimes with unexpected, wonderful results. A classic case involves a 70-year-old accountant who suffered a stroke to the left side of his brain. He then began noticing colors and scenery for the first time in his life. He became an artist—painting pictures that sold in a museum!

What Is Creativity?

Creativity is best defined as the ability to produce unconventional ideas. Those ideas may be workable and practical or speculative and idealistic. The creativity of an idea is not judged by its brilliance but instead by its uniqueness and diversity. How creative are you?

The Creativity Test

The following questions can provide you with some information about your level of creativity. For those questions that are timed, use a stopwatch or other accurate timepiece.

You need a piece of paper and a pen or a pencil for some questions. Do not use software or reference materials, and be sure to work alone.

Begin Test

1. Quick! In two minutes, make a list of all the uses you can think of for a 12-inch piece of string.

2. Now, think of all the uses for a lightbulb. Timing is again two minutes.

Answer true or false to the following:

3. I believe that most people take life too seriously.　　T　　F

4. I like to write poetry and/or short stories.　　T　　F

5. I have been described by others as unconventional or eccentric.　　T　　F

6. You're trapped in a square. What is the best way to get out?

    ❏ Remember what I learned about tricky escapes.

    ❏ Become a cube and "rise to the occasion."

7. I can easily see more than one solution to a problem.　　T　　F

8. I have much trouble focusing on repetitive or boring tasks.　　T　　F

End Test

See Appendix A for scoring directions.

The following chart describes your level of creativity.

Score	Classification	Suggestions
9–10	Creative Genius	Invent something new.
7–8	Excellent Creativity	You're innovative.
5–6	Good Creativity	You're open to new ideas.
3–4	Creative Potential	Bring out your creativity.
1–2	Low Creativity	Look around.
0	Stuck in the Box	Become a cube. It's your only hope to climb out of the box.

Here are some exercises to improve the functioning of your left brain:

◆ Each night before you go to bed, list three things you *must* do the next day. Designate them as *a*, *b*, and *c*. Try not to end the day without *a* being done, and do *not* begin *b* until *a* is done.

◆ Next time you don't know how to do something, resist the urge to ask someone else until you have spent at least 30 minutes researching the topic alone via the Internet, reading, and so on.

◆ Spend just 10 minutes every day reading about a subject you've always thought was boring. Stay on task without interruption, then try to recall what you read.

Here are some exercises to improve the functioning of your right brain:

◆ Sketch people or nature scenes that you observe.

◆ Make an attempt to assemble a household object, toy, or something else without referring to the directions.

◆ Get involved with a team project and work collaboratively rather than alone.

Here are some exercises to help both sides of your brain work together:

◆ Brainstorm and criticize. Come up with as many solutions to a problem as possible in five minutes. Write these solutions on a piece of paper without judging them—no matter how impractical the idea may seem. Then, look at each idea and judge its pros, cons, and overall merit.

◆ Do some type of different activity each day. Vary your routine. If you're the type who *must* go out every Friday night, stay home instead. Conversely, if you prefer to stay home often, get out and socialize.

◆ Practice balance in your lifestyle. If you're a big spender, try being thrifty for a week.

◆ When you're confronted with a problem, think about how another person—someone who has a different personality type from yours—would handle it. You can do this in your head or in reality (depending on the situation).

Memory and Concentration

In This Chapter

◆ Take the Short-Term Memory Test

◆ Explore factors that affect short-term memory

◆ Explore several types of long-term memory measures

◆ Learn about exercises and activities for memory improvement

Memory is divided into long-term and short-term abilities. You need to remember what you have just learned today, as well as recollect information learned many years ago.

Short-Term Memory Test and Exercises

The ability to remember newly learned material for a short period of time is an important factor in intelligence because it allows you to complete any new problem-solving operation. The material can then be transferred into your long-term memory for future retrieval in dealing with similar problems. Or, alternately, the newly learned material may be discarded ("forgotten") if not needed in the future.

> **Words to the Wise** _____
>
> Without short-term memory, there can be no new additions to long-term memory. If a person's short-term memory has been wiped out by excessive drug use, accidental brain injury, or dementia, he or she cannot learn anything new. Seems like one's short-term memory is worth protecting!

Short-Term Memory Test

Try these questions to see how well you remember information that you just learned.

Begin Test

1. Say the following words aloud: clock, toy, baby, water, clown, dog, umbrella, chair, lightbulb, bed. Turn to your scrap paper and write as many as you can remember without looking. Then, go to the next question before scoring.

2. Say the following numbers aloud: 43, 286, 58, 37, 525, 65, 88. Turn away. Write them on your scrap paper.

3. Say the following numbers aloud: 5, 9, 8, 6, 3. Turn away. Write them *backward* on scrap paper.

4. Say the following words aloud: pencil, football, stove, ruler, glove. Turn away. Write them *backward* on scrap paper.

5. Say the following numbers aloud: 7, 13, 94, 25, 62. Turn away. Write them *backward* on scrap paper.

6. Say the following words aloud: platoon, sailboat, airplane, theater, kitchen, automobile, television. Turn away. Write them *backward* on scrap paper.

7. What is the name of this test? (No cheating.)

8. In what numbered question was the word *glove?* (Don't look back.)

9. In what question was number *94?*

End Test

See Appendix A for answers.

The following chart will show where you stand in relation to others on the Short-Term Memory Test.

Short-Term Memory Test—Results and Interpretation

Total Score	IQ Range	Classification	Percentile
12–15	130	Very Superior	98
9–11	115–129	Superior	85–98
6–8	100–114	High Average	50–84
3–5	85–99	Low Average	15–49
1–2	70–84	Borderline Deficient	2–14
0	<70	Deficient	<2

Here are some factors affecting short-term memory:

◆ Emotional states (such as anxiety, depression, and irritability)

◆ Fatigue

◆ Attention and concentration problems

◆ Noise and distraction

◆ Drug or alcohol use

Caution

If any of these factors apply during a test of short-term memory, it might be wise to disregard the results and retake the test when you are free from any type of interference.

Exercises for Improving Short-Term Memory

The following list contains numbers with a rhyming object. Visualize the object associated with each number.

one gun	six sticks
two shoe	seven heaven
three key	eight gate
four door	nine wine
five hive	ten hen

Now here are 10 objects:

1. chair	6. pencil
2. suitcase	7. car
3. desk	8. book
4. mirror	9. computer
5. glass	10. phone

Your task is to picture each of these 10 objects interacting in some way with the rhyming object that corresponds with its number. For example, because chair is number one, picture a chair with a gun on top of it.

Allow yourself 60 seconds to perform this association task. Use a stopwatch or other appropriate timer because timing must be exact. When you're finished, write all 10 objects *in order* on your scrap paper.

I'll bet that you got 9 or 10 correct. This is probably an improvement on your performance on the Short-Term Memory Test.

More Short-Term Memory Exercises

Feeling confident? Ready to try another 10 objects? All right ... let's go!

1. bottle	6. cat
2. magazine	7. rock
3. flashlight	8. basket
4. spoon	9. pillow
5. scissor	10. flower

And you thought the *last* exercise was difficult! This time, write all 10 objects *backward*. You may number 1 to 10 on your scrap paper, but write the last object first—and soon!

What happened? Don't tell me it was easier. I'm sure it was, because that's what happens when you use this type of association to remember things. Now you know how to trick your brain into remembering better. More brain tricks will appear in later chapters.

Did You Know?

Short-term memory tests are excellent measures of intellectual ability apart from any prior learning or experience.

Words to the Wise

If you know anyone who uses marijuana and claims that it's harmless, ask that person one question: "How has your memory been lately?"

Long-Term Memory Tests and Exercises

Information that's learned throughout the course of life is stored in your long-term memory. People who have higher intelligence will have a better ability to pick up new facts and store them mentally for future recall.

General Knowledge Test

The following questions measure your store of general knowledge acquired during your lifetime. Pick the best answer.

> **Caution**
>
> Because general knowledge is acquired over a *lifetime*, if you are college-age or younger, this test may provide a low estimate of your long-term memory. Keeping that in mind, you may wish to use it for fun and practice only.

Begin Test

1. Typical hands have how many fingers each?

    a. 5   b. 10   c. 2   d. 20

2. What happened between 1914 and 1918?

    a. The American Revolution

    b. World War II

    c. World War I

    d. The Battle of the Bulge

3. How many bones are in the human body?

    a. 209   b. 206   c. 203   d. 210

4. What trophy is given out at the Academy Awards?

    a. Grammy   b. Oscar   c. Emmy   d. Vega

5. The six-pointed star is the Star of:

    a. David   b. the North   c. Gabriel   d. Rufus

6. What are leukocytes?

    a. platelets   b. free radicals
    c. red blood cells   d. white blood cells

7. Popination refers to:

    a. the manufacturing of hashish and marijuana

    b. fertility treatments

    c. bar-hopping

    d. psychodrama

8. How many breaths does the average person take per day?

    a. 10,500   b. 128,000   c. 50,000   d. 23,000

End Test

See Appendix A for the answers.

The following chart will show you where you stand in relation to others regarding long-term memory general information.

General Knowledge Test–Results and Interpretation

Number Correct	IQ Range	Classification	Percentile
8	130	Very Superior	98
6–7	115–129	Superior	85–98
5	100–114	High Average	50–84
3–4	85–99	Low Average	15–49
2	70–84	Borderline Deficient	2–14
0–1	<70	Deficient	<2

 Caution

Long-term memory tests rely on strong (American) English knowledge of words and facts. If you lack this background, take these tests for fun and practice rather than as a true measure of your long-term memory.

Vocabulary Test

Vocabulary is one of the best measures of overall intelligence because it's unaffected by visual handicaps, motor difficulties, or even minor brain injury or deterioration. Vocabulary is the only score on traditional IQ tests that increases steadily with age. Because it takes higher intelligence to understand subtle differences among words (and therefore use them correctly), a good vocabulary symbolizes high abstract reasoning as well as good long-term memory.

Begin Test

1. Choose the word that is most similar to the word *fastidious:*

   a. sloppy   b. careful   c. insightful   d. scary

2. Choose the word that is most similar to the word *mundane:*

   a. quiet   b. ordinary   c. exotic   d. unreasonable

3. Choose the word that is most similar to the word *disobedient:*

   a. loud   b. honest   c. rebellious   d. refined

4. Choose the word most nearly opposite in meaning to the word *indict:*

   a. absolve   b. accuse   c. malign   d. establish

5. Pick the synonym for the word *acquisition:*

   a. surrogate   b. routine   c. procurement   d. execution

6. Pick the synonym for the word *municipal:*

   a. proliferate   b. penalize   c. stimulate   d. metropolitan

7. Pick the antonym for the word *hindrance:*

   a. interruption   b. benefit   c. obstacle   d. barrier

8. Pick the antonym for the word *silent:*

   a. humble   b. tranquil   c. vociferous   d. hushed

9. Pick the synonym for the word *raucous:*

   a. gluttonous   b. voracious   c. discordant   d. bewitching

10. Pick the synonym for the word *short:*

    a. blemish   b. vociferate   c. effulgent   d. curtailed

End Test

See Appendix A for the answers.

The following chart will help you calculate your score for the long-term memory vocabulary test.

Vocabulary Test—Results and Interpretation

Number Correct	IQ Range	Classification	Percentile
9–10	140	Very Superior	99.9
7–8	130–139	Very Superior	98–99.8
5–6	120–129	Superior	90–97
4	110–119	High Average	78–89
3	100–109	Average	50–74
2	90–99	Average	25–49
0–1	<90	Below Average	<25

If you got 4 out of 10 of these difficult words right, you scored in the high-average range on this measure.

This score placed you above 75 to 89 percent of the population with a long-term memory IQ between 110 and 119.

Personal Data Test

A common frustration that occurs when attempting to test your long-term memory is the fact that most tests require educational background and familiarity with the test language—that is, until now.

The Personal Data Long-Term Memory Test tests just that: personal historical facts. Just how well do you know yourself?

The following questions should be easy, right? They pertain to you and your own life. Let's see how well you do. Use a piece of paper and a pen or a pencil but *no* software, reference materials, or help from anyone else. After you finish, score your answers and see how well you did at knowing yourself and your immediate world. Use a stopwatch or other timepiece to ensure exact timing where needed.

Begin Test

1. In two minutes, write the names of seven family members' birthdays. I'll be kind and tell you to only write the month and day and forget about the year.

2. In two minutes write the phone numbers of seven friends.

3. What is your license plate number? Alternately, if you don't drive, what is the license plate number of one person who usually drives you places?

4. What is your country dialing code?

5. What was the name of your third-grade teacher?

6. What is your mom and dad's (or whoever played that role) middle names?

7. In two minutes write the first and last names of 10 neighbors.

8. In two minutes name seven characters from your favorite book *or* television show.

End Test

See Appendix A for the scoring instructions.

> **Did You Know?**
>
> For years, mental health professionals have used what is called "Oriented x3" as a major part of a mental health status exam. This exam is important because it can be used to determine whether or not someone needs to be hospitalized, is competent to manage his or her own money, and so on. What the "x3" stands for is *time*, *place*, and *person*. Here are some examples: "What day is today?", "What city are we in?", and "Why are you here?"

The following chart will show you where you stand in relation to others on the long-term memory personal data test.

Personal Data Test—Results and Interpretation

Total Score	IQ Range	Classification	Percentile
12–14	130	Very Superior	98
9–11	115–129	Superior	85–98
6–8	100–114	High Average	50–84
3–5	85–99	Low Average	15–49
1–2	70–84	Borderline Deficient	2–14
0	<70	Deficient	<2

Long-Term Memory Exercises

Here are some exercises for improving your long-term memory:

◆ Observe your surroundings and write a summary of what you saw and heard.

◆ Read a variety of materials and test yourself on recall.

◆ Associate new words and phrases with information you already know and store in place in your brain.

◆ Use as many senses as possible to recall events: visual, auditory, touch, smell, taste, and so on.

Chapter 7

Unique Talent Tests

In This Chapter

- ◆ Explore your performance in specific areas of human ability
- ◆ Discover your special talents
- ◆ Learn the implications of certain types of giftedness
- ◆ Become aware of exercises and activities to improve your performance in all areas

Talent is defined as the unique ability to do something especially well. What are your talents? The tests in this chapter are self-report measures of your experience, ability, and interest in activities that may provide some indication of your special areas of giftedness. Because the measures rely on your own responses, it's important that you work alone and answer each question honestly. Because the results are only for your own knowledge and interest, you should wish to obtain an accurate score.

Musical IQ Test: Am I the Next Mozart or a Famous Rock Star?

For each of the following questions, circle the alternative that most clearly describes you. If the statement applies to you all the time, circle *a* (true). If the statement applies to you most of the time, circle *b* (mostly true). If the statement rarely applies to you, circle *c* (mostly false). If the statement never applies to you, circle *d* (false). There is no time limit on this test.

Begin Test

1. When you listen to the radio, do you "channel flip" until you find a song that you like?

   a   b   c   d

2. Can you play two or more musical instruments?

   a   b   c   d

3. Do you often sing along when you hear music?

   a   b   c   d

4. When you watch a movie or video, do you listen to and remember the background music?

   a   b   c   d

5. Do certain songs remind you vividly of people or places from the past?

   a   b   c   d

6. Does music have the power to change your mood?

   a   b   ċ   d

7. When you hear upbeat music, do you start moving or dancing to it?

   a   b   c   d

8. Can you hear a piece of music for the first time and immediately know whether you like it or not?

   a   b   c   d

9. Do you observe and remember subtle differences between different types of music?

   a   b   c   d

10. Have you ever attempted to write or succeeded in writing a piece of music?

    a   b   c   d

End Test

Scoring and Interpreting Musical IQ Test Results

For the answers, see Appendix A.

Did You Know? _____

Beethoven was completely deaf toward the end of his life—when he composed his greatest pieces.

The following chart describes your musical interest and talent:

Musical IQ Test—Results and Interpretation

Score	Classification	Suggestions
9–10	Musical Genius	Line up a recording contract!
7–8	Talented at Music	Develop your talent and it may lead you to a great place.
5–6	Musically Inclined	Music is an important part of your life.
3–4	Musical Talent not Forefront	Keep the music in the background.
1–2	Little or No Musical Awareness	You must be more of a "techie" or visual person.
0	Tone Deaf	Clean out your ears!

Tips for Improving Your Musical IQ

◆ Listen closely to several different types of music (for example, classical, rock, and country). Try to make note of the similarities and differences among them.

◆ Learn to play an instrument that you have never played.

◆ Pay attention to music played during movies, TV shows, and videos.

◆ Sing along and practice moving to the beat when you hear music being played.

Visual IQ Test: Will My Artwork Sell in a Museum?

For each of the following questions, circle the alternative that most clearly describes you. If the statement applies to you all the time, circle *a* (true). If the statement applies to you most of the time, circle *b* (mostly true). If the statement rarely applies to you, circle *c* (mostly false). If the statement never applies to you, circle *d* (false). There is no time limit on this test.

Begin Test

1. When you hear a story, do you see the characters and their actions vividly in your mind's eye?

   a   b   c   d

2. Do you often doodle while sitting and passing time?

   a   b   c   d

3. Have you ever thought that you could redecorate someone's house or office so that it would be much more appealing?

   a   b   c   d

4. When someone asks directions or asks for a description of a place, do you draw maps and pictures?

   a   b   c   d

5. When you are driven somewhere, do you remember how to get there automatically the next time?

   a   b   c   d

6. When you walk down the street, do you hold your head up and notice the people and places around you?

   a   b   c   d

7. Do you sometimes sketch people or scenic views when you have the opportunity to observe them?

   a   b   c   d

8. Do you remember the colors and scenery in your dreams?

   a   b   c   d

9. Do others compliment you on your decorating ability or artwork?

   a   b   c   d

10. Have you ever received a prize or award for your artwork?

   a   b   c   d

End Test

Scoring and Interpreting Visual IQ Test Results

For the answers, see Appendix A.

The following chart describes the meaning of your score on the Visual IQ Test:

Visual IQ Test—Results and Interpretation

Score	Classification	Suggestions
9–10	Creative Artist	Tell the museum to put in an early bid!
7–8	Talented in Art	Consider decorating, commercial art, and advertising or graphic design.

continues

Visual IQ Test—Results and Interpretation   (continued)

Score	Classification	Suggestions
5–6	Good Artist	You do the layout or party decorations.
3–4	Art Isn't Your Thing	You're better at verbal or tech work.
1–2	You Must Dislike Art	Heed the above advice, but try to visualize for practice.
0	Can't Draw a Straight Line with a Ruler	There's hope. (Neither can this writer!)

Words to the Wise

If you're talented in art, music, drama, or something else, do you have the financial backing to support your passion? If not, I suggest either a secondary "practical" job or (if possible) a way to commercialize your talent to finance your pursuit in its true form.

Tips for Improving Your Visual IQ

◆ Make a serious attempt to notice your surroundings. When you get the chance, try to redraw from memory some of the things you've seen.

◆ Sketch nature scenes and pictures of friends. You may make someone quite happy with a personal drawing.

◆ Draw maps instead of using verbal directions.

Verbal IQ Test: Will I Become a Great Speaker?

For each of the following questions, circle the alternative that most clearly describes you. If the statement applies to you all the time, circle *a* (true). If the statement applies to you most of the time, circle *b* (mostly true). If the statement rarely applies to you, circle *c* (mostly false). If the statement never applies to you, circle *d* (false). There is no time limit on this test.

Begin Test

---

1. I write letters to people often because I enjoy doing so.

   a   b   c   d

2. When I hear something, I can usually repeat it accurately.

   a   b   c   d

3. I know the words to most of my favorite songs.

   a   b   c   d

4. I enjoy reading.

   a   b   c   d

5. I can hold my own during a conversation with intelligent people.

   a   b   c   d

6. People often choose me to speak for the group.

   a   b   c   d

7. When I am upset I can easily verbalize what is bothering me.

   a   b   c   d

8. I have received compliments from others about how articulate I am.

   a   b   c   d

9. I have been a member of a debate team or speakers' group.

   a   b   c   d

10. When I give directions or describe a room, I use words more easily than pictures.

    a   b   c   d

End Test

Scoring and Interpreting Verbal IQ Test Results

For the answers, see Appendix A.

The following chart describes your verbal ability and interest results:

Verbal IQ Test—Results and Meaning

Score	Classification	Suggestions
9–10	Special Way with Words	Become a great orator or writer.
7–8	Good Command of Language	Words come easily to you.
5–6	Verbal—Good Speaker	Teaching, dealing with the public, and sales are good careers for you.
3–4	Average Verbal Ability	You read and speak adequately when necessary.
1–2	Not a Wordsmith	You prefer nonverbal types of expression.
0	Very Quiet Type	You speak only when spoken to!

Tips for Improving Your Verbal IQ

◆ Set a goal to learn and use one new word per day.

◆ Read everything. Reading tabloids or comic books still provides practice and is better than not reading at all.

◆ Volunteer to make a speech or introduce someone at your next work or social meeting.

◆ Describe things you see with as many words as you can think of.

Mechanical IQ Test: Am I a Genius in Figuring Out How Things Work?

For each of the following questions, circle the alternative that most clearly describes you. If the statement applies to you all the time, circle *a* (true). If the statement applies to you most of the time, circle *b* (mostly true). If the statement rarely applies to you, circle *c* (mostly false). If the statement never applies to you, circle *d* (false). There is no time limit on this test.

Begin Test

1. When things break, do you fix them yourself rather than replace them or have someone else fix them?

   a   b   c   d

2. Do you know where to find the appropriate tool when you need it?

   a   b   c   d

3. Do other people bring you broken objects, knowing that you may be able to repair them?

   a   b   c   d

4. If you wanted to know how something worked, would you take it apart rather than read the directions?

   a   b   c   d

5. Do you carry tools in your car or have them at your desk in case you need them? (A needle and thread are also considered tools.)

   a   b   c   d

6. Do you assemble gadgets easily—often without much help from verbal or written directions?

   a   b   c   d

7. Would you feel safer on a bicycle that you made yourself versus one that you bought at a reputable store?

   a   b   c   d

8. Does your make-do or quick repair (of an object, vehicle, article of clothing, and so on) often last a very long time?

   a   b   c   d

9. You would rather make an article of clothing or a piece of furniture as opposed to buying it.

   a   b   c   d

10. When you observe a broken object, do you automatically make a move to fix it?

    a   b   c   d

End Test

Scoring and Interpreting the Mechanical IQ Test Results

For the answers, see Appendix A.

The following chart describes your mechanical interests and abilities:

Mechanical IQ Test—Results and Meaning

Score	Classification	Suggestions
9–10	Mechanical Genius	Become an inventor!
7–8	Excellent Mechanic	You can fix anything.
5–6	Mechanically Inclined	You're often the tool guy/girl.
3–4	You Dislike Mechanical Tasks	Read the instructions!
1–2	You're Not Mechanically Inclined	Bring it to the repair shop.
0	Mechanically Clueless	If it ain't broke, don't touch it or it *will* be!

Tips for Improving Your Mechanical IQ

- Take apart an old gadget and reassemble it.

- Assemble a toy or piece of furniture with minimal use of directions.

- Observe and ask questions when you bring your car, bicycle, or something else to the repair shop. See whether you can remember and name the parts and their functions.

Psychomotor IQ Test: Will I Become a Star Athlete?

For each of the following questions, circle the alternative that most clearly describes you. If the statement applies to you all the time, circle *a* (true). If the statement applies to you most of the time, circle *b* (mostly true). If the statement rarely applies to you, circle *c* (mostly false). If the statement never applies to you, circle *d* (false). There is no time limit on this test.

def•i•ni•tion

Psychomotor pertains to the motor effects of psychological processes. Performance in this area usually depends upon coordination between visual and motor abilities.

Begin Test

1. Physical risk thrills and excites me.

   a   b   c   d

2. I do not enjoy sitting still for long time periods.

   a   b   c   d

3. I can learn most sports by practice, without any formal training.

   a   b   c   d

4. I am often the leader in physical activities.

   a   b   c   d

5. I have a natural sense of coordination.

   a   b   c   d

6. In school, I was one of the first people chosen for sports teams.

   a   b   c   d

7. Since I was young, I was usually stronger, faster, and more energetic than my peers.

   a   b   c   d

8. Coaches and recruiters have shown special interest in me for at least one sport.

   a   b   c   d

9. My physical reflexes are sometimes quicker than my mind.

   a   b   c   d

10. I have given serious thought to becoming a professional athlete.

   a   b   c   d

End Test

>) **Words to the Wise**
>
> Becoming a serious athlete is no game. It involves a *lot* of hard work. Be prepared for hours of rigorous training and routines that don't leave room for much else. Regardless of natural talent, *practice* and *discipline* are required to make it to the big leagues.

Scoring and Interpreting Your Psychomotor IQ Test Results

For the answers, see Appendix A.

The following chart describes the meaning of your score on the Psychomotor IQ Test:

Psychomotor IQ Test—Results and Interpretation

Score	Classification	Suggestions
9–10	Star Athlete	Get your agent and sign your contract!
7–8	Great Hope	It's the minor leagues for you—and with luck and practice, who knows?
5–6	Good in Sports	You're an asset to the home team.
3–4	Adequately Athletic	Play for fun.
1–2	Not the Athletic Type	You're getting a workout, anyway!
0	You Hate Sports	Remember: it's only a game!

Tips for Improving Your Psychomotor IQ

◆ Take up a new sport. Read about it, take lessons, and practice. Do whatever it takes to train your mind and body in the right moves.

◆ Walk, work out, and keep in shape. This way you will make friends despite your lack of skill when playing a competitive sport.

◆ Practice yoga or ballet (now recommended for football players!). Try activities that provide good counterbalance to what you normally do.

Caution

Be sure to have a thorough medical examination and obtain clearance from a physician before embarking on any new, strenuous physical activity program.

Mathematical IQ Test: Am I a Mathematical Genius?

For each of the following questions, circle the alternative that most clearly describes you. If the statement applies to you all the time, circle *a* (true). If the statement applies to you most of the time, circle *b* (mostly true). If the statement rarely applies to you, circle *c* (mostly false). If the statement never applies to you, circle *d* (false). There is no time limit on this test.

Begin Test

1. Math is/was my favorite subject in school.

   a b c d

2. I have always been fascinated by numbers.

   a b c d

3. When the restaurant check comes, my friends hand it to me to search for errors and figure out the tip.

   a b c d

4. I can do math problems in my head.

a   b   c   d

5. I am skilled at managing money.

a   b   c   d

6. I have an unusual ability to remember dates and numbers.

a   b   c   d

7. During my free time, I often play number games.

a   b   c   d

8. I can foresee financial problems more quickly than others can.

a   b   c   d

9. I like to play the stock market, gamble, or work at a job that involves handling money.

a   b   c   d

10. I have been elected or appointed treasurer of a club or organization.

a   b   c   d

End Test

Scoring and Interpreting Your Mathematical IQ Test Results

For the answers, see Appendix A.

The following chart describes the meaning of your score on the Mathematical IQ Test:

Mathematical IQ Test—Results and Interpretation

Score	Classification	Suggestions
9–10	Mathematical Genius	Einstein, watch out!
7–8	Excellent in Math	You're the resident mathematician.
5–6	Good in Math	You handle the finances.

Score	Classification	Suggestions
3–4	Average Math Skills	You can handle everyday math demands.
1–2	Math Isn't Your Favorite Subject	Let someone else do the finances!
0	No Math for You!	Count on your fingers.

Tips for Improving Your Mathematical IQ

♦ Volunteer to handle money for your club or workplace. (This is usually not the most desirable job.)

♦ Play number games of increasing difficulty. You may actually begin to look forward to doing them.

♦ Practice adding numbers and performing duties involving math without the use of software. Do whatever mathematical operations can be done in your head.

Did You Know?

Einstein flunked eighth-grade math before he went on to develop his higher mathematical theories. Guess he was bored with everyday academic subjects!

Chapter 8

Tests for Specific Knowledge

In This Chapter

- ◆ Learn about your knowledge in special areas of human interest
- ◆ Explore work-related, academic, social, and life skills
- ◆ Become aware of where you stand on acquired knowledge and interest in certain areas
- ◆ Consider suggestions for improving your knowledge in various subjects

Previous chapters have demonstrated the relationship between intellectual *ability* and academic or work-related *aptitudes*. The important difference focuses on what is innate versus what is acquired. Similarly, while Chapter 7 explored *talent*, this chapter explores *knowledge* in specific areas of human interest. The following tests should be taken alone, without the help of software or reading material. This will ensure your most accurate score.

Will I Get Rich? Take the Money IQ Test

For each of the following questions, circle the alternative that most clearly describes you, your beliefs, or your behavior in most situations. There is no time limit on this test.

Begin Test

1. Your first million will probably come from:

    a. Winning a reality TV show

    b. A lottery ticket

    c. Working really hard

    d. Working smart and working hard

2. Which statement best describes your financial situation?

    a. I plan far ahead for a rainy day.

    b. I'm always hit with surprise expenses.

    c. I borrow frequently.

    d. My finances are sometimes good, sometimes bad.

3. Where are you most likely to shop?

    a. At high-end boutiques or department stores

    b. At average-priced, large stores

    c. At small stores

    d. At thrift and discount shops

4. If you ask a bank for a loan, what would be its likely response?

    a. "Who can co-sign?"

    b. "Sure—you have great credit."

    c. "What?"

    d. "Ha. That's funny."

5. The best alternative here is that money buys:

   a. freedom

   b. power

   c. security

   d. all of the above

6. Interest is:

   a. Something the bank talks about

   b. Something I have in my date or partner

   c. A good way to earn on money I saved

   d. Who knows?

7. If someone asks for a loan:

   a. I usually say, "Yes."

   b. I carefully consider whether I can afford it.

   c. I carefully consider whether the person is likely to pay me back on time.

   d. b and c

8. If I had a sudden windfall, I would:

   a. Give most of it away.

   b. Invest in high-risk ventures to make it grow.

   c. Spend it on lavish surroundings, a vacation, and clothes.

   d. Invest in safe investments and go on living my current lifestyle.

9. The best thing about a rich family is:

   a. I would never have to work.

   b. I could enjoy many luxuries.

   c. I would get a head start toward making my own fortune.

   d. I could meet a rich mate much more easily.

10. The best thing about credit cards is:

    a. I can buy now and pay later.

    b. I don't have to notice the expense immediately.

    c. I can use them in an emergency.

    d. I don't need to carry much cash.

End Test

Scoring and Interpreting Your Money IQ Test Results

For the answers, see Appendix A.

The following chart will help you interpret your score on the Money IQ Test:

Money IQ Test—Results and Interpretation

Score	Classification	Suggestions
9–10	Excellent Money Knowledge	You're on the road toward wealth.
7–8	Good with Money	You are the resident money manager.
5–6	Balance Money with Other Goals	You probably won't run into money trouble.
3–4	Not That Interested in Money	Try to see the importance of money to yourself and to others.
1–2	Money is a Necessary Evil	You need money to live, so take care of it!
0	I Never Have Any of That Stuff	Get a piggy bank!

Tips for Improving Your Money IQ

◆ Save 10 percent of your gross income even if you can't afford it. This is why forced pension plans work.

◆ Comparison shop at various stores and buy only what you need.

◆ Ask yourself, "Do I really want this vacation, dinner, article of clothing, and so on?" (This technique really works.)

◆ Place money in stocks or funds that are difficult to sell so you're denied immediate access.

Words to the Wise

Real success is not how much money you earn but how much money you keep. Think about that the next time you're tempted to go on a spending spree.

Do I Have What It Takes to Run My Own Business? Entrepreneur's IQ Test

For each of the following questions, circle the alternative that most clearly describes you, your beliefs, or your behavior in most situations. There is no time limit on this test.

Begin Test

1. How many times have you been fired from a job?

   a. never

   b. once

   c. twice

   d. more than twice

2. How were/are your parents employed?

   a. municipality or corporation

   b. small business

   c. one was self-employed

   d. both were self-employed

3. What would be your primary reason to start your own business?

   a. to be my own boss

   b. to make more money than working for someone else

   c. to have more time off

   d. to have an outlet for creative ideas

4. How far did you get (or do you plan to get) in school?

   a. some high school

   b. high school

   c. college degree

   d. Master's degree or doctorate

5. Your relationship with the parent who provided most of the family income was:

   a. competitive

   b. strained

   c. comfortable

   d. nonexistent

6. Your work career has been mostly in:

   a. small business (1–100 employees)

   b. medium business (101–500 employees)

   c. large business (more than 500 employees)

   d. a public service agency

7. On whom do you rely for business advice?

   a. your employees

   b. outside advisors

   c. internal management teams

   d. only yourself

8. If you gambled, you would place a bet on:

   a. a small chance to make a killing

   b. a favorite

   c. a 2-to-1 shot

   d. a 10-to-1 shot

9. You work better:

   a. with a team

   b. with one person

   c. alone

   d. in a large office

10. You hate to discuss:

    a. employee problems

    b. expense accounts

    c. new practices

    d. the future of the business

End Test

---

def•i•ni•tion

An **entrepreneur** is a person who organizes, operates, and assumes the risk for a business venture.

Scoring and Interpreting Your Entrepreneur's IQ Test Results

For the answers, see Appendix A.

The following chart will help you interpret your score on the *Entrepreneur's* IQ Test:

Entrepreneur's IQ Test—Results and Interpretation

Score	Classification	Suggestions
9–10	Donald Trump Would Hire You	Get on *The Apprentice!*
7–8	Entrepreneur	You prefer to be your own boss.
5–6	Will Work for Others at the Beginning	Get a job first, then start a business.
3–4	Prefer to be Employed By Others	Manage a business rather than own one.
1–2	Job Security a Must	Line up a job with a good pension.
0	Security Only	High-security prison may be the answer!

Did You Know? _____

A new business doesn't have to be capital intensive. Some of the most successful corporations began as basement-type enterprises (think Mary Kay Cosmetics and Fred Smith's FedEx). Keep your overhead low.

Tips for Improving Your Entrepreneur's IQ

◆ Start your own business from a hobby. Find friends who will pay you to sew, build furniture, and so on.

◆ Get advice from reputable nonprofit, small-business advisors.

◆ Remember that you can make your own hours as an entrepreneur, so you may be able to work easily around existing home and work demands.

Words to the Wise _____

One viewpoint about "paid hobbies" is that real success is *getting paid* to do what you would *pay* to do. And if the passion is there, a paid hobby can become a very lucrative business indeed. However, because many new businesses fail, remember to invest only what you can afford to lose.

> **Caution**
>
> Be wary of any advertisements on the Internet or in publications that request money for investment advice or start-up capital. Reputable small-business advisors don't ask for money up front and provide you with proper credentials. If it sounds too good to be true, it probably is.

Will I Be a Great Scientist? Take the Science IQ Test

For each of the following questions, circle the correct answer. There is no time limit on this test.

Begin Test

1. How many cranial nerves does your body have?

   a. 301   b. 12   c. 52   d. 36

2. What does the pancreas do?

   a. fights germs

   b. absorbs glucose from the bloodstream

   c. produces bile

   d. releases insulin into the bloodstream

3. The pleura is part of the:

   a. lungs   b. heart   c. tongue   d. teeth

4. At what rate does the adult heart beat per minute?

   a. 100–130 beats per minute

   b. 12–16 beats per minute

   c. 60–90 beats per minute

   d. 120–140 beats per minute

5. HIV can be transmitted from an infected person to a noninfected person by:

   a. handshakes

   b. blood only

   c. breastmilk and semen only

   d. vaginal fluid, blood, semen, and breastmilk

6. Rods and cones are part of the:

   a. heart   b. eye   c. stomach   d. ovaries

7. Which bone is not in the leg?

   a. fibula   b. tibia   c. femur   d. ulna

8. Who is the top predator of the sea?

   a. dolphin   b. killer whale
   c. tiger shark   d. my science teacher

9. Which of the following animals uses supersonic radar to catch its prey?

   a. elephants   b. foxes
   c. bats   d. my English teacher

10. If a nuclear bomb exploded and radiation went through the city, which of the following animals would be most likely to survive?

    a. dogs   b. cockroaches   c. elephants   d. my math teacher

---

End Test

Scoring and Interpreting Your Science IQ Test Results

For the answers, see Appendix A.

The following chart will help you interpret your score on the Science IQ Test:

Science IQ Test—Results and Interpretation

Score	Classification	Suggestions
9–10	Great Scientist	Put your scientific talent to good use.
7–8	Love Science	Work in a science field.
5–6	Good at Science	Balance science with your other interests.
3–4	Adequate Scientist	You have a beginning interest in science.
1–2	Science Isn't Your Favorite Subject	Study liberal arts.
0	What Is That Strange Subject About?	Stay away from the lab. You might blow the place up!

Tips for Improving Your Science IQ

◆ Read pocket dictionaries; descriptions are in lay terms.

◆ Read about new discoveries in health and science magazines.

◆ Watch The Discovery Channel and other TV programs that explain complex scientific concepts in simple terms.

◆ Read science fiction for fun, but circle the facts against reality.

Am I a Good Historian? Take the History IQ Test

For each of the following questions, circle the correct answer. There is no time limit on this test.

Begin Test

1. Another name for medieval times was:

   a. Dark Ages   b. Middle Ages   c. Renaissance   d. Pax Romana

2. Which was founded in 1492?

   a. Australia   b. America   c. India   d. South Africa

3. Who was the first king of France?

   a. Attila   b. Pepin   c. Alaric   d. Clovis

4. Which king of England was beheaded?

   a. Charles I   b. Charles II   c. Charles III   d. Charles IV

5. Where did Ferdinand Magellan die?

   a. Philippines   b. Spice Island   c. Japan   d. Australia

6. Which of the following first united China in history?

   a. Lu Bu Wei   b. Yin Zheng   c. Xiang Yu   d. Lui Bei

7. Where is the longest river?

   a. Costa Rica   b. Canada   c. Africa   d. China

8. Who said, "I have just begun to fight"?

   a. George Patton   b. John Adams
   c. John Paul Jones   d. Hang Sui

9. Who created communism in Russia?

   a. Karl Marx   b. Joseph Stalin
   c. Mikhail Gorbachev   d. Vladimir Lenin

10. Who was the head of the Greek pantheon?

   a. Hera   b. Gaia   c. Cronus   d. Zeus

End Test

Scoring and Interpreting Your History IQ Test Results

For the answers, see Appendix A.

The following chart will help you interpret your score on the History IQ Test:

History IQ Test—Results and Interpretation

Score	Classification	Suggestions
9–10	Historian	Become a politician.
7–8	You Know Your History	Tie the past in with today.
5–6	Average Historical Knowledge	Keep your balance between *then* and *now*.
3–4	Not Much Interest in the Events of Yesterday	Open your mind to the past.
1–2	You Shun the Past; What's Hot for You Is *Now*	Don't shun the past; learn from it.
0	What Is History?	History repeats itself, so it may have something to offer you.

Tips for Improving Your History IQ

◆ Read classical literature. You may be surprised at the similarity between human experiences then and now.

◆ Watch The History Channel and The Learning Channel.

◆ Get a hold of some middle-grade history books. They're easy and fun reading.

Am I Entertainment Savvy? Take the Entertainment IQ Test

For each of the following questions, circle the correct answer. There is no time limit on this test.

Begin Test

1. What is Spider-Man's real name?

   a. John Sagitas   b. Tom Cruise   c. Peter Parker   d. Tyrone Bunder

2. Which pretty woman's first born were twins?

    a. Julia Roberts   b. Kate Hudson
    c. Angelina Jolie   d. Jennifer Garner

3. What does "The O.C." stand for?

    a. Orange Creek   b. Over Cast
    c. Open Corner   d. Orange County

4. Which Oscar winner was born in South Africa?

    a. Nicole Kidman   b. Halle Berry
    c. Charlize Theron   d. Reese Witherspoon

5. What is Road Runner's first name?

    a. Mimi   b. Cyndy   c. Luann   d. Daisy

6. Complete the cartoon title: Barney and …

    a. Folks   b. Boys   c. Friends   d. Us

7. Who starred in the movie *E.T.?*

    a. Drew Barrymore   b. Tatum O'Neil
    c. Kate Hudson   d. Shannen Doherty

8. Jennifer Lopez owns a:

    a. boutique   b. horse farm   c. studio   d. restaurant

9. What is the name of the singer who is known for her big breasts?

    a. Pamela Anderson   b. Britney Spears
    c. LeAnn Rimes   d. Dolly Parton

10. Do you think this writer watches all of these TV shows and performances?

    a. Yes—or you wouldn't be writing about them.

    b. Sometimes.

    c. Rarely, but you catch up by reading about them.

    d. Never! You've got to be kidding!

End Test

Scoring and Interpreting Your Entertainment IQ Test Results

For the answers, see Appendix A.

The following chart will help you interpret your score on the Entertainment IQ Test:

Entertainment IQ Test—Results and Interpretation

Score	Classification	Suggestions
9–10	High Entertainment IQ and Much Focus on Pop Culture	Become an entertainment reporter and get paid to watch TV and go to movies!
7–8	You Enjoy TV and Movies	You have a good knowledge of what's hot and what's not.
5–6	An Average Knowledge of Pop Culture	You balance pop culture with other areas of knowledge.
3–4	Some Acquaintance with Entertainment	Read and watch videos and TV more for fun.
1–2	Not Interested in Pop Culture	You're not a TV and movie fan.
0	You Just Aren't Into Entertainment of a Fad Nature	Get some pop culture in you. You might enjoy it.

Tips for Improving Your Entertainment IQ

◆ Watch TV shows that summarize the entertainment events of the day (for example, *Entertainment Tonight, Access Hollywood, The Insider, Inside Edition*, and E!).

◆ Watch special events where celebrities gather (for example, The Academy Awards, The Cannes Film Festival, the MTV Music Awards, and so on).

◆ Read the tabloids. They are easy reading and cover various subjects quickly.

Am I a Food Connoisseur? Take the Food IQ Test

For each of the following questions, circle the alternative that most clearly describes you, your beliefs, or your behavior in most situations. There is no time limit on this test.

Begin Test

1. At a barbecue, you eat:

   a. everything

   b. vegetables and fruit

   c. meat mostly

   d. snacks and fries

2. If you could bring any food to a party, you would choose:

   a. meat   b. pasta   c. vegetables   d. dessert

3. Which category of food storage is best for eating?

   a. fresh   b. frozen   c. canned   d. pickled

4. Do you often have problems with food spoilage or overdue expiration dates?

   a. No. I use everything in a timely manner.

   b. Sometimes.

   c. Often; I buy more than I need.

   d. Always. I'm a chef, not a food inspector.

5. When you dispose of food, where do you put it?

   a. In the compost bin where it can be used as fertilizer.

   b. In the trash where no one can eat it.

   c. Where the animals can eat it

   d. In my mouth; I never throw food away.

6. Which type of food storage is most likely to cause botulism?

   a. fresh   b. frozen   c. canned   d. dehydrated

7. What is feijoada made from?

   a. black beans and meat

   b. soybeans

   c. corn and milk

   d. goat's milk

8. What is hominy made from?

   a. beans   b. corn   c. milk   d. carrots

9. What are Japanese soba noodles made from?

   a. buckwheat   b. milk and eggs
   c. whole-wheat bread   d. corn

10. Which food in this group is the lowest in calories?

    a. 5 ounces of M&M's

    b. 5 ounces of yogurt traisi

    c. 1 fat-free pretzel

    d. 15 assorted olives

End Test

Scoring and Interpreting Food IQ Test Results

For the answers, see Appendix A.

The following chart will help you interpret your score on the Food IQ Test:

Food IQ Test—Results and Interpretation

Score	Classification	Suggestions
9–10	Food Connoisseur	Get your own cooking show.
7–8	Hot Cook	Invite me for dinner!

continues

Food IQ Test—Results and Interpretation

Score	Classification	Suggestions
5–6	Cool Cook	You know what's in, but you seek shortcuts to save time.
3–4	You Cook to Eat	Splurge on a good restaurant when you want to treat someone.
1–2	Don't Want to Bother	Order takeout!
0	Hate to Cook	Hire a cook or marry a chef!

Tips for Improving Your Food IQ

◆ Read the labels on food products. Next time you go grocery shopping, see what everyday edibles are made from. You may be surprised.

◆ Explore new restaurants. Ask questions if you don't understand an item on the menu.

◆ Buy cookbooks and read them.

◆ Watch cooking shows. There are certainly enough of them.

> **Words to the Wise**
>
> My mother always said, "If you can read, you can cook." Follow recipes step by step, and you will produce a good-tasting meal. No more excuses!

How Well Do I Know Sports? Take the Sports IQ Test

For each of the following questions, circle the correct answer. There is no time limit on this test.

Begin Test

1. In football, what is the origin of the word *quarterback?*

   a. The highest-paid players in the early days of football were paid a quarter of the team's collective salary.

   b. The quarterback was positioned one quarter of the way between the linemen and the fullback.

   c. The ideal throwing motion was considered to be a quarter of the way back behind the ear.

   d. Fans used to throw quarters at these players in displays of admiration for especially strong performances.

2. Why is the Los Angeles baseball team called the "Dodgers"?

   a. Players once used baseball as a means to try and avoid being drafted into the military.

   b. It's named after the first owner of the team, Jonus Dodge.

   c. The team's original home, Brooklyn, had many trolleys on its streets that pedestrians had to dodge.

   d. It was originally a minor-league team from Dodge City, Kansas.

3. What does Shaquille O'Neal's first and middle name (Shaquille Rashau) mean in Islam?

   a. Thunder Strength   b. Courageous Heart
   c. Little Hero   d. Little Warrior

4. What is the origin of the word "coach"?

   a. Kocchus, the legendary trainer of athletes in ancient Greece

   b. The village of Kocs, Hungary—the birthplace of the horse-drawn carriage

   c. Cochise, the fearless nineteenth-century leader of the Chiricahua Apache

   d. The medieval Latin word *coccus*, an imitation of a rooster's crow

5. Modern pentathlon comprises five events: shooting, running, fencing, and what else?

    a. cycling and archery

    b. swimming and show jumping

    c. sailing and walking

    d. swimming and walking

6. Which team won four World Cups?

    a. Italy   b. Brazil   c. Germany   d. Argentina

7. Which golfing legend has been a runner-up at The Open a record seven times?

    a. Tom Watson   b. Seve Ballesteros
    c. Jack Nicklaus   d. Arnold Palmer

8. How many serves is a player allowed in a game of tennis?

    a. There is no limit   b. 4   c. 12   d. 16

9. If a football player from the other team catches the ball, what is it called?

    a. fumble   b. intercept   c. interest   d. interception

10. What is the origin of the word *gymnastics?*

    a. Latin for "bone breaker"

    b. Greek for "to train naked"

    c. From an original Olympic event called a "gymno," which was a predecessor to the pommel horse

    d. From an Old English term for "flexible"

End Test

Scoring and Interpreting Your Sports IQ Test Results

For the answers, see Appendix A.

The following chart will help you interpret your score on the Sports IQ Test:

Sports IQ Test—Results and Interpretation

Score	Classification	Suggestions
9–10	Armchair Athlete of the Year	Become a sports commentator.
7–8	Knowledgeable in Sports	You're the one to ask if we miss the game.
5–6	Usually Up on Important Sports News	You can hold your own when the conversation turns to sports.
3–4	Aware of Major Sports Figures and Events	Other subjects interest you more.
1–2	Barely Know What's Happening in the Sports World	Learn the basics and you may become interested.
0	Sports? What Sports?	You're too busy playing to watch ... right?

Tips for Improving Your Sports IQ

◆ Watch games. Ask questions. Once you understand a sport, you can enjoy watching it.

◆ Play sports trivia games.

◆ Watch ESPN and the end of just about every news program on TV or radio.

◆ Read the sports section of the newspaper.

Will I Live a Long and Healthy Life? Take the Health IQ Test

For each of the following questions, circle the correct answer. There is no time limit on this test.

1. Which of the following is the greatest cause of fatigue?

   a. excessive physical exertion

   b. inadequate sleep for several days

   c. emotional stress

   d. low caloric intake

2. Which of the following is *not* a good reason to stretch before exercising?

   a. Stretching increases your general coordination.

   b. Stretching relaxes your body.

   c. Stretching encourages upper-diaphragm breathing.

   d. Stretching warms your muscles.

3. Perspiring heavily during a workout means:

   a. You lose water weight only.

   b. You lose fat and water weight.

   c. It may be very humid in your workout location.

   d. You are less healthy than someone who perspires less.

4. Which of the following, per serving, is highest in cholesterol-producing saturated fat?

   a. butter   b. olive oil   c. safflower oil   d. fish oil

5. Which of the following is *not* one of the functions of protein?

   a. It breaks down into glucose.

   b. It regulates biochemical reactions.

   c. It is needed for the growth and repair of body tissues.

   d. It insulates the body, protecting organs and nerve pathways.

6. Strengthening my abdominal muscles is one of the best ways to:

    a. lose fat in my abdominal region

    b. attract men or women

    c. ensure better breathing

    d. protect against back pain

7. Which of the following exercises is an example of aerobic activity?

    a. push-ups   b. weight training

    c. meditation   d. walking

8. Alcohol metabolizes at a rate of about:

    a. one drink per hour

    b. two drinks per hour

    c. depends on the person's tolerance

    d. one drink per 50 pounds per hour

9. Which of the following is *not* included in the class of nutrients that humans need to survive?

    a. fats   b. water   c. vitamins   d. meats

10. You have been lifting weights for 6 months. Three times per week, you do 10 repetitions with 20-pound weights. It used to be difficult, but now it takes little or no effort. You now should:

    a. increase the amount of reps

    b. increase the weight

    c. stop exercising because you met your goal

    d. increase to five times per week for weight training

End Test

Scoring and Interpreting Your Health IQ Test Results

For the answers, see Appendix A.

The following chart will help you interpret your score on the Health IQ Test:

Health IQ Test—Results and Interpretation

Score	Classification	Suggestions
9–10	You Do All the Right Things	You should live forever!
7–8	You Know What's Healthy, but Sometimes You Deviate	Stay on track and you'll feel better.
5–6	Good Health Awareness. You Follow Health Rules When Convenient	Set up a regular program and stick to it.
3-4	Sometimes Other Things Come Before Healthy Behavior	Remember the cliché: "Health is your greatest possession."
1–2	You Probably Think of Your Health Only When It Fails	Do the right thing and you'll get sick less often.
0	Why Worry About Health? You've Got to Die From Something!	You must be young. Think of the future; you want to keep feeling healthy!

Tips for Improving Your Health IQ

◆ Get a thorough medical examination *before* you feel sick. Focus on *prevention* before you need treatment.

◆ Get into a healthy routine, including proper sleep, healthful food, and exercise. Once you begin, you will *feel* the difference between healthy and unhealthy behavior. This will motivate you to stick with it.

◆ Watch the Discovery Health Channel. Read health-oriented magazines. There is much information out there, so utilize it.

Chapter 9

Testing Your Child's IQ

In This Chapter

◆ Administer the Children's Aptitude Test to your preschool or school-age child

◆ Score and interpret results for the Children's Aptitude Test

◆ Learn how to improve your child's intellectual and academic functioning

◆ Address serious concerns and explore resources

"How smart is my child?" Every parent asks this question at some point. This chapter provides you with two instruments to measure ability: the first for children ages 3 to 6, and the second for children ages 7 to 15. You'll be able to see your child's profile by scoring and interpreting the test results. This can then point you in the direction for possible improvement and enrichment opportunities for your child.

Children's Aptitude Test—3 to 6 Years

Read the following questions to your child. Then, present the possible answers one at a time. Record your child's responses by circling the answer that was given. Don't assist your child or give him or her the answers during the testing. You may review the correct answers *after* you finish testing. Remember, this information is only for your own knowledge—so you want to have an accurate, independent performance. There is no time limit for this test.

Caution

As always, the tests in this book are for information and entertainment purposes only. If you have concerns about your child's intellectual functioning, be sure to contact an appropriate medical, mental health, or educational specialist.

Begin Test

1. 4 + 3 = ?

    a. 6   b. 1   c. 7   d. 9

2. If I have five oranges and I give two to my friend, how many oranges do I have left?

    a. 7   b. 4   c. 8   d. 3

3. 1, 2, 3, ___, 5, 6

    Which number belongs in the blank space above?

    a. 7   b. 2   c. 4   d. 5

4. How old are you?

    a. 1, 2   b. 7 or older   c. child   d. 3, 4, 5, or 6

5. How many fingers are on both hands?

    a. 5   b. 10   c. 2   d. 15

6. A ___ C D E

    Which letter belongs in the blank space?

    a. F   b. T   c. D   d. B

7. I can eat:

    a. rocks   b. paper   c. water   d. apples

8. Which is not real?

    a. chickens   b. dogs   c. ghosts   d. fish

9. Which does not belong with the others?

    a. mother   b. father   c. sister   d. teacher

10. A dog and a cat are alike in some way. A dog and a cat are alike
    because they are both:

    a. fruit   b. vegetables   c. animals   d. people

11.

    Which picture below is the same as this (point to the above figure)?

    a.    b.

    c.    d.

12.

Which picture below is the same as this (point to the above figure)?

a.

b.

c.

d.

13.

Which picture below is the same as this (point to the above figure)?

a.

b.

c.

d.

14.

Which picture below is the same as this (point to the above figure)?

a.

b.

c.

d.

15.

Which picture below is the same as this (point to the above figure)?

a.

b.

c.

d.

Point to the following pictures and ask your child, "Is this a(n)?". State each alternative one by one. If your child answers "Yes" to more than one choice, tell him or her that there can be only one right answer and that he or she must only choose one.

16.

a. cat

b. dog

c. elephant

d. giraffe

17.

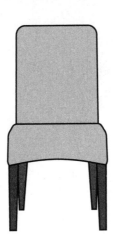

    a. table

    b. refrigerator

    c. chair

    d. desk

18.

    a. shoe

    b. sock

    c. hand

    d. foot

19.

    a. elephant

    b. bird

    c. owl

    d. snake

20.

    a. apple

    b. pear

    c. grapes

    d. orange

End Test

Scoring and Interpreting Test Results

For the answers, see Appendix A.

Score ____

> **Caution**
> The younger the child, the more likely that other factors such as fatigue, mood, immaturity, and distractibility can interfere with obtaining a high test score. You may want to re-administer the test at a later date to compare scores if you feel that your child may not have performed at his or her full potential.

The following chart will help you calculate your child's IQ score:

IQ Equivalents of Test Scores for Children Ages 3 to 6 Years

	Age			
Score	**3**	**4**	**5**	**6**
19–20	140	140	135	130
17–18	130	130	125	120
15–16	125	120	115	115
13–14	120	115	110	110
11–12	115	110	105	100
9–10	110	100	100	100
7–8	105	95	100	95
5–6	100	90	95	95
3–4	95	90	95	90
1–2	90	85	85	80
0	90	80	80	80

IQ Score ____

Now that you have obtained your child's IQ score, the following chart will enable you to see where he or she stands in relation to his or her peers.

Classification and Percentile Ranks for IQ Scores

IQ Score	Classification	Percentile
140	Genius	99.9
130–139	Very Superior	98–99.8
120–129	Superior	90–97
110–119	High Average	75–89
100–109	Average	50–74
90–99	Low Average	25–49
80–89	Below Average	10–24
70–79	Borderline	3–9
70	Deficient	2

For example, if your child got 12 questions correct, he or she obtained an IQ score of 105—which places him or her at the average level and above 50 to 74 percent of his or her peers.

As you can see, most IQ scores fall within the average range, with very low and very high scores a somewhat rare occurrence.

Once again, as in previous chapters, you may observe the way in which IQ scores are distributed throughout the general population.

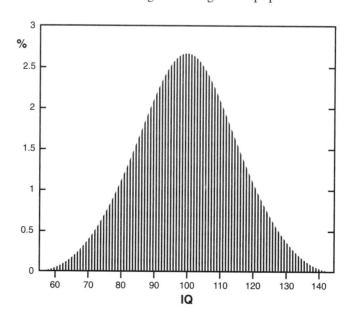

Tips to Improve Aptitude in Younger Children

The following measures can have a significant effect on intellectual development in children ages three to six years:

- ◆ Educational enrichment. Place your child in programs with gifted and talented children.

- ◆ Early exposure to books and learning materials.

- ◆ Approach problems from several angles, considering many possibilities rather than one solution.

- ◆ Good nutrition. There's definitely truth behind the ideas that you can't think on an empty stomach and "you are what you eat."

- ◆ Adequate rest. Give your child's brain the opportunity to rejuvenate in order to be at his or her best when absorbing new learning and integrating old skills.

Children's Aptitude Test—7 to 15 Years

This test consists of 40 questions measuring verbal as well as nonverbal skills.

Find a place free of distractions and sit with your child to assist him or her as needed. With younger children, you may need to read the directions; older children should be able to follow the test directions with less assistance. It's important to let your child work alone without the assistance of software or other aids. Do not give him or her the answers or any clues. Remember, this information is only for your own knowledge. There is no time limit for this test.

Begin Test

1. Which comes next in the following series:

   A C D F G I ...

   a. K   b. J   c. H   d. M

2. 4, 8, 10, 20, 22, 44 ...

   a. 56   b. 88   c. 46   d. 34

3. B X D V F T ...

    a. G   b. H   c. Q   d. R

4. 1, 3, 7, 13, 21 ...

    a. 25   b. 28   c. 26   d. 31

5. B C D F G H J K L M N ...

    a. O   b. P   c. Q   d. R

6. What is the square root of 36?

    a. 6   b. 24   c. 3   d. 9

7. What is 11 multiplied by 11?

    a. 122   b. 131   c. 121   d. 111

8. What is the cube root of 64?

    a. 16   b. 4   c. 8   d. 24

9. Say these numbers after me:

    6 5 2 1 4

    a. correct   b.–d. incorrect

10. Say these numbers backward:

    4 6 3 5

    a. correct   b.–d. incorrect

11. Say these letters after me:

    T A D E C

    a. correct   b.–d. incorrect

12. Say these letters backward:

    A L B M

    a. correct   b.–d. incorrect

13. If these words were placed in alphabetical order, which would come first?

    a. squeeze   b. sneeze   c. sleaze   d. trapeze

14. In the previous example, which word would come third alphabetically?

    a. squeeze   b. sneeze   c. sleaze   d. trapeze

15. How many f's are in the following sentence?

    Which of the f's fall first?

    a. 3   b. 2   c. 4   d. 5

16. Which word means the same as *need?*

    a. enjoy   b. desire   c. despise   d. require

17. Which word means the opposite of *inept?*

    a. happy   b. skillful   c. positive   d. miserable

18. How many states are in the United States?

    a. 48   b. 52   c. 40   d. 50

19. Which is the largest ocean in the world?

    a. Atlantic   b. Pacific   c. Indian   d. Arctic

20. Who wrote *Romeo and Juliet?*

    a. Hemingway   b. Wolfe   c. Shakespeare   d. Voltaire

21. ☐ is to ■ as ◯ is to ?

    a. ◯

    b. ●

    c. ⊠

    d. ▲

22.   is to   as   is to ?

   a.   b.

   c.   d.

23.

   a.   b.

   c.   d.

Which one of the above designs is least like the others?

   a.   b.   c.   d.

24. —   ⟨   ✕

Which comes next?

a.

b.

c.

d. +

25. +   ✱   =

a. ✱

b. ✳

c. ✳

d. ✳

26.

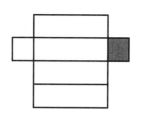

folded makes

a.

b.

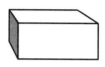

c.

d.

27.

 + =

a.

b.

c.

d.

28.   – (minus)   =

a.

b.

c.

d.

29.

folded makes

a.

b.

c.

d.

30.

Which comes next in the above series?

a.

b.

c.

d.

31.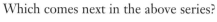

Which comes next in the above series?

32.

Which comes next in the above series?

33.

Which comes next in the above series?

a.

b.

c.

d.

34. Which of the following designs does not belong with the others?

a.

b.

c.

d.

35.

Which figure below completes the above matrix?

a.   b.

c.   d.

36. Which of the following figures is least like the others?

a.   b.

c.   d.

37.

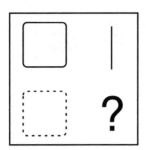

Which figure below completes the above matrix?

a.

b. - - - - - -

c.

d.

38.

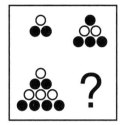

Which figure below completes the above matrix?

a.

b.

c.

d.

39.

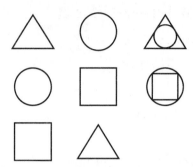

Which figure below completes the above matrix?

a.
b.

c.
d.

40.

Which figure below completes the above matrix?

a.
b.

c.
d.

End Test

Scoring and Interpreting Test Results

For the answers, see Appendix A.

Verbal Test Score (questions 1–20) _____

Nonverbal Test Score (questions 21–40) _____

The following chart will help you calculate your child's verbal IQ score:

IQ Equivalents of Verbal Test Scores for Each Age Level–7 to 15

	Age								
Score	**7**	**8**	**9**	**10**	**11**	**12**	**13**	**14**	**15**
19–20	150	150	145	140	135	135	130	130	130
17–18	145	145	140	135	130	125	125	125	125
15–16	140	135	135	130	130	125	125	120	120
13–14	135	130	130	125	125	120	120	120	115
11–12	130	125	120	115	110	105	100	100	100
9–10	125	120	115	115	110	105	100	100	100
7–8	120	115	115	110	105	100	100	95	95
5–6	110	105	100	100	100	95	95	90	90
3–4	100	100	95	95	95	90	90	90	85
1–2	90	90	85	85	80	80	80	75	70
0	80	80	80	80	70	70	70	70	70

Verbal IQ Score _____

The following chart will help you calculate your child's nonverbal test score:

IQ Equivalents of Nonverbal Test Scores for Each Age Level–7 to 15

	Age								
Score	**7**	**8**	**9**	**10**	**11**	**12**	**13**	**14**	**15**
19–20	150	145	140	135	130	130	130	130	130
17–18	140	140	135	135	130	130	130	125	125

continues

IQ Equivalents of Nonverbal Test Scores for Each Age Level–7 to 15 (continued)

	Age								
Score	7	8	9	10	11	12	13	14	15
15–16	130	130	130	125	120	120	115	110	110
13–14	125	125	125	120	115	115	110	110	105
11–12	120	120	115	110	110	110	100	100	100
9–10	110	110	110	105	100	100	100	100	100
7–8	100	100	100	100	100	100	95	95	90
5–6	95	95	95	95	95	95	95	90	90
3–4	90	90	90	90	90	90	90	90	85
1–2	85	80	80	80	80	80	80	80	80
0	70	70	70	70	70	70	70	70	70

Nonverbal IQ Score ____

To obtain the total IQ score for your child, add the verbal IQ score to the nonverbal IQ score and divide the result by two.

For example, if your child obtained a verbal IQ score of 106 and a nonverbal IQ score of 98, add 106 + 98 and divide the result (204) by 2 to obtain a total IQ score of 102.

Formula: Verbal IQ Score ____ + Nonverbal IQ Score ____

= ____ ÷ 2

= Total IQ Score ____

Refer to the "Classification and Percentile Ranks for IQ Scores" table earlier in this chapter to understand which category your 7- to 15-year-old falls into and where he or she stands in relation to his or her peers. For example, if your 9-year-old obtained a total score of 115, he or she is functioning in the high-average intellectual range. This means that he or she scored higher than 75 to 89 percent of his or her peers. Refer to the bell curve on page 141 to observe the distribution of IQ scores throughout the general population. The majority of children's and adult IQ scores fall within the middle range.

Tips to Improve Aptitude in Older Children

Your school-age child may benefit intellectually and academically by pursuing some of the following activities:

◆ Read, read, read. You can always increase knowledge in specific areas as well as overall reading ability through exposure to books and other reading materials.

◆ Encourage problem-solving ability. Rather than give your child the answers, teach him or her to research and problem-solve through available sources.

◆ Become aware of and encourage your child to participate in advanced placement and enrichment programs available through the school.

◆ Encourage healthy eating, adequate rest, and avoidance of chemicals to ensure optimal brain function.

If You Have Concerns About Your Child's Score ...

If your child's intellectual or academic functioning appears to be less than expected (based upon test results or school performance), it may be time to obtain a professional opinion. The success of early-intervention programs provides much evidence for the ability to correct deficiencies and improve intellectual functioning in children. Therefore, you—as a parent—should not delay in consulting with medical and educational specialists as well as psychologists to determine how to maximize your child's intellectual functioning.

Chapter 10

Can You Really Raise Your IQ?

In This Chapter

- ◆ Practice exercises designed to strengthen brainpower
- ◆ Enjoy solving complex math and logic puzzles
- ◆ Stretch your imagination and reasoning abilities
- ◆ Improve your ability to recognize and win at mind games

The brain is like a muscle. With proper use and training, it can be strengthened. The exercises in this chapter are designed to help you firm up your brain muscle while engaging in enjoyable activities. What a good workout at the gym does for your body, a good workout with this book does for your brain. Get on the treadmill—and have fun!

The solutions and explanations for all the problems in this chapter can be found in Appendix A.

For the following problems, find the correct answers. We are *really* testing your brain in this chapter because most questions are *not* multiple choice. This means that you must generate the answer solely from your own mind.

> ### Words to the Wise
> The ability to recognize the correct answer is much greater than the ability to remember it. This is because there are more cues. Next time you can't remember something, try to recall facts related to it. This will jar your memory by increasing cues.

Brain Teasers

Here are the *real* tests!

Hidden Gold

There's a bar of solid gold waiting for you behind one of four doors. You have one chance to choose the correct door. The following statements provide cues to help you choose. Additionally, you know that two of the statements are true while two of the statements are false. Which door hides the treasured bar of gold?

> Door 1: Enter and get the gold.
>
> Door 2: You won't find any gold here.
>
> Door 3: Stay away. No gold.
>
> Door 4: The statement on Door 1 is false.

Money Marbles

In a certain culture, marbles are used as money. Different colors are worth different amounts. One green marble is worth two yellow marbles and one red marble. One yellow marble is equal to two blue marbles. Two blue marbles are equal to five black ones. One black marble is worth as much as four red marbles. How many red marbles is a green marble worth?

4s and 9s

Without using any software, answer the following question: are there more 4s or more 9s in all the numbers between 1 and 70,000?

Students

1. Maria does well in math but not French. John does well in English and math. Colleen does well in English but not math. Mike does well in French but not English. If each student studies two of the three subjects, who is most similar to John?

2. At a certain college, the students can only choose from two majors: engineering or communications. Students are allowed to major in both. If there are 600 students at the college and 75 percent are communications majors while 10 percent are engineering majors, how many students are majoring in both subjects?

3. Five students took a psychology exam. Zoe scored higher than April, who did not have the highest score. Eileen had the highest score, and Mike scored higher than Tom but lower than Zoe. Who had the lowest score?

4. Which two statements are necessary to make the first sentence true?

    100 students took the test.

    a. Forty answered fewer than half the questions.

    b. Twenty students failed the test.

    c. At least half the questions were answered by 60 students.

    d. Eighty students were successful.

Socks and Clocks

1. Jason has 58 black socks and 42 dark-blue socks in his drawer. Without turning on the light, he can make sure he has found a matching pair by pulling out how many socks?

    a. 3   b. 5   c. 4   d. 7

2. Ted has 34 red socks, 46 blue socks, and 21 green socks. How many socks must he pull out of the drawer in the dark to ensure that he has found a matching pair?

3. There are four socks in a drawer. Carol closes her eyes and tries to pick two that are the same color. The choices are two red socks, one black sock, and one white sock. Carol's first pick is a red sock. When she closes her eyes and picks a second sock, what are the chances that she will pick the other red sock?

4. You have two clocks. One is completely broken and does not move at all. The other clock is one hour slow. Which has the greatest number of times when it's correct?

5. My watch was 10 minutes fast, and the meeting that should have begun at 2 P.M. began at 2:30. What time was it on my watch when the meeting began?

Buses and Planes

1. Imagine that you're a bus driver and you go 4 miles east, then 24 miles north, 54 miles west, and 13 miles south. What is the name of the bus driver?

2. There are seven girls on a bus.

   Each girl has seven backpacks.

   In each backpack, there are seven big cats.

   For every big cat, there are seven little cats.

   Question: how many legs are there in the bus?

3. You're on an airplane that travels 3,000 miles in 4 hours with a tail-wind and 3,000 miles in 5 hours with a headwind. How long would it take you to travel 1,000 miles on the same airplane with no wind?

Fenced In

You have 497 feet of fence that must be placed in a straight line around the back of your restaurant. If a fence post is placed at every 7 feet of fence, how many fence posts are needed? (Careful—this question is a bit tricky.)

Logic Puzzles

Now try the following logic puzzles.

Necessary Statements

In the following questions, which two statements are necessary to make the sentence at the beginning of the questions true?

1. José is playing football.

   a. José is on the football team.

   b. Everyone in the park is playing football.

   c. José is in the park.

   d. Football is played in the park.

2. John is taller than Fred.

   a. Beanstalk is the tallest.

   b. John is the tallest.

   c. John is as tall as Beanstalk.

   d. Beanstalk is taller than Fred.

Love Logic

If Mike likes Jane more than Susan, Zelda more than Holly, and Holly more than Jane, which of the following is *not* true?

   a. He likes Susan more than Zelda.

   b. He likes Zelda more than Susan.

   c. He likes Holly more than Susan.

   d. He likes Zelda more than Jane.

Math-a-Logic

1. In the following addition, each of the letters A, B, C, D, and E represents one of the numbers from 1 to 5 (equal letters represent equal numbers, and different letters represent different numbers). The first and last numbers of the sum are given. What must each letter's value be to get the final sum? What number is missing, and what is the sum?

    ABCDE
    DABEC
    EAABC
    ACDAE
    + _____
    9CBA0

2. Again, equal letters represent equal numbers and different letters represent different numbers. Using the values for letters you obtained earlier, what must each of the following numbers be? What is the missing number, and what is the sum?

    ABCABA
    BBDCAA
    ABEABB
    ABDBAA
    + _____
    AAFGBDH

3. 33 555 8888 is to 88 555 3333 as 666 55555 7777777 is to:

    _____

Appendix A

Answers to Chapter IQ Tests

Answers to Chapter 1

1. c. neat
2. a. energetic
3. d. obedient
4. b. wise
5. c. usually

6. d. 0
7. b. 15
8. c. H
9. d
10. c. Wright
11. c. fruit (mango)
12. c. peculiar (peril)
13. a. captain (apt)
14. c. illness (pneumonia)
15. b. cynical
16. d. 32
17. c. 2
18. c. 29
19. a. 42
20. d. 24
21. b. Talia
22. b. Thursday
23. c. gabs
24. c. grandmother
25. a. Marcia

26. c. glass—all others are metal
27. c. Rome—all others are countries
28. d. hat—all others can be polished
29. b. 24—all others are odd numbers
30. a. left top line slants downward—others slant upward
31. c
32. d
33. b
34. b
35. d
36. c
37. c
38. a
39. d
40. a
41. b. 62
42. d. 144
43. d. 25
44. b. 126
45. d. 84
46. b. 13
47. b. 8
48. a. Cromwell to Allehan
49. c. same speed
50. d. 5 miles

Give yourself one point for each correct answer. Then compute your total number of correct responses.

Total number correct ____

Answers to Chapter 2

Give yourself one point for each correct answer.

Vocabulary	Pattern Recognition	Verbal Reasoning	Mathematical Reasoning	Logic
1. c	6. d	11. c	16. d	21. b
2. a	7. b	12. c	17. c	22. b
3. d	8. c	13. a	18. c	23. c
4. b	9. d	14. c	19. a	24. c
5. c	10. c	15. b	20. d	25. a
Total ___	Total ___	Total ___	Total ___	Total ___

Classification	Short-Term Memory	Spatial Ability	Mathematical Computation	Visual-ization
26. c	31. c	36. c	41. b	46. b
27. c	32. d	37. c	42. d	47. b
28. d	33. b	38. a	43. d	48. a
29. b	34. b	39. d	44. b	49. c
30. a	35. d	40. a	45. d	50. d
Total ___	Total ___	Total ___	Total ___	Total ___

Answers to Chapter 3

Paired–Item Memory IQ Test

1. d	6. a
2. a	7. b
3. b	8. b
4. c	9. c
5. b	10. d

Give yourself one point for each correct response. Then compute your total number of correct answers.

Total number correct ___

Nonverbal Abstract Reasoning IQ Test

1. c	6. a
2. a	7. c
3. d	8. d
4. d	9. d
5. b	10. b

Each correct answer is worth one point. Compute your total number of correct responses.

Total number correct ___

Pattern Recognition IQ Test

1. a	6. d
2. b	7. a
3. c	8. b
4. a	
5. d	

Score one point for each correct answer. Then compute your total correct responses.

Total number correct ___

Mazes IQ Test

1. Maze Number 1

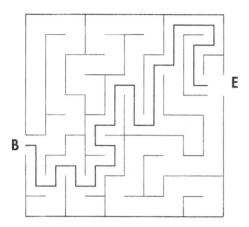

2. Maze Number 2

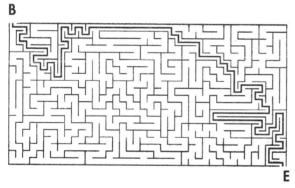

3. Maze Number 3

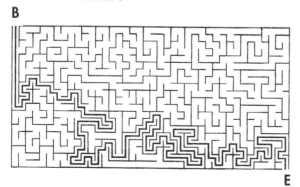

4. Maze Number 4

B

E

5. Maze Number 5

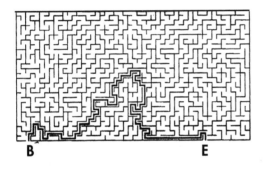

B   **E**

Answers to Chapter 4

Language Arts Test

1. a	6. d	11. b	16. a	21. b	26. d
2. b	7. a	12. a	17. d	22. b	27. b
3. c	8. a	13. a	18. c	23. d	28. a
4. b	9. d	14. d	19. d	24. c	29. b
5. c	10. d	15. b	20. b	25. c	30. b

Each correct answer is worth one point. Compute your total number of correct responses.

Total number correct _____

Mathematical Achievement Test

1. b (the first coin is a *quarter*, not a nickel)	5. a
2. d	6. c—7 is the only prime number
3. c	7. c
4. b	8. b

Give yourself one point for each correct answer. Then compute your total number of correct responses.

Total number correct _____

Acuity Skills Test

1. a	6. b	11. b	16. c
2. b	7. c	12. b	17. c
3. d	8. a	13. d	18. c
4. d	9. b	14. b	19. c
5. a	10. d	15. d	20. a

Each correct answer is worth one point.

Total number correct _____

Spatial Skills Test

1. a	6. b
2. a	7. d
3. c	8. c
4. d	9. a
5. c	

Score one point for each correct answer. Then compute your total correct response.

Total number correct _____

Mechanical Skills Test

1. b	5. c
2. c	6. d
3. b	7. a
4. b	8. a

Give yourself one point for each correct response and compute your number of correct answers.

Total number correct _____

Visual-Motor Speed Test

4	6	1	3	9	4	7	8	6	0	3	1	5	6	2	9	1	0	4	2
J	A	X	M	Z	J	B	T	A	Q	M	X	E	A	C	Z	X	Q	J	C
3	8	0	4	6	2	1	7	5	8	6	4	2	8	1	6	9	5	1	3
M	T	Q	J	A	C	X	B	E	T	A	J	C	T	X	A	Z	E	X	M
8	6	4	1	6	9	0	5	3	2	7	8	0	9	4	6	3	5	0	6
T	A	J	X	A	Z	Q	E	M	C	B	T	Q	Z	J	A	M	E	Q	A
6	5	2	9	5	7	1	6	4	8	9	2	1	7	8	3	2	4	1	9
A	E	C	Z	E	B	X	A	J	T	Z	C	X	B	T	M	C	J	X	Z
1	9	8	7	3	4	2	0	6	1	2	8	5	0	6	7	1	2	9	8
X	Z	T	B	M	J	C	Q	A	X	C	T	E	Q	A	B	X	C	Z	T

Each correct answer is worth one point. Score 1–100.

Total ____

Answers to Chapter 5

Brain Type Test

Scoring Directions for Brain Type Test:

Questions 1–10: Give yourself one point for every *a*, two points for each *b*, three points for each *c*, and four points for each *d*.

Score ___

Questions 11–20: Give yourself four points for each *a*, three points for each *b*, two points for each *c*, and one point for each *d*.

Score ___

Add both scores: total score ____

Creativity Test

1. 4 or less: 0 points

   5–9: 1 point

   more than 10: 2 points

2. 4 or less: 0 points

   5–9: 1 point

   more than 10: 2 points

3. T: 1 point, F: 0 points

4. T: 1 point, F: 0 points

5. T: 1 point, F: 0 points

6. a: 0 points, b: 1 point

7. T: 1 point, F: 0 points

8. T: 1 point, F: 0 points

Total score ____

Answers to Chapter 6

Short-Term Memory Test

Question	Number Correct	Points
1.	0–3	0
	4–7	1
	8–10	2
2.	0–1	0
	2–4	1
	5–7	2
3.	0–1	0
	2–3	1
	4–5	2
4.	0–1	0
	2–3	1
	4–5	2
5.	0–1	0
	2–3	1
	4–5	2
6.	0–2	0
	3–5	1
	6–7	2

7. correct: 1 point

   answer: Short-Term Memory Test

8. correct: 1 point

   answer: question 4

9. correct: 1 point

   answer: question 5

Add the total points you obtained for each correct answer.

Total score _____

Long-Term Memory Test—General Knowledge

1. a	5. a
2. c	6. d
3. b	7. c
4. b	8. d

Give yourself one point for each correct answer. Then compute your total number of correct responses.

Total correct ____

Long-Term Memory Test—Vocabulary

1. b	6. d
2. b	7. b
3. c	8. c
4. a	9. a
5. c	10. d

Each correct answer is worth one point.

Total number correct ____

Personal Data Long-Term Memory Test

Question	Number Correct	Points
1.	0–1	0
	2–4	1
	5–7	2
2.	0–1	0
	2–4	1
	5–7	2

continues

continued

Question	Number Correct	Points
3.	0	0
	1	1
4.	0	0
	1	1
5.	0	0
	1	1
	2	2
6.	0–1	0
	2–4	1
	5–7	2
7.	0–1	0
	2–4	1
	5–7	2
8.	0–1	0
	2–4	1
	5–7	2

Total score _____

Answers to Chapter 7

Musical IQ Test

Give yourself one point for every *a* or *b* and 0 points for every *c* or *d*.

Total score _____

Visual IQ Test

Score one point for each *a* or *b* and 0 points for each *c* or *d*.

Total score _____

Verbal IQ Test

Each *a* or *b* is worth one point. Each *c* or *d* is worth 0 points.

Total score _____

Mechanical IQ Test

Score one point for each *a* or *b* answer and 0 points for each *c* or *d* answer.

Total score _____

Psychomotor IQ Test

Give yourself one point for every *a* or *b* and 0 points for every *c* or *d*.

Total score _____

Mathematical IQ Test

Each *a* or *b* answer is worth one point. Each *c* or *d* answer is worth 0 points.

Total score _____

Answers to Chapter 8

Money IQ Test

1. d	6. c
2. a	7. d
3. d	8. d
4. b	9. c
5. d	10. d

Give yourself one point for each correct answer and compute your total number of correct responses.

Total number correct _____

Entrepreneur's IQ Test

1. d	6. a
2. d	7. d
3. d	8. a
4. c	9. c
5. c	10. b

Give yourself one point for each correct answer and compute your total number of correct responses.

Total number correct _____

Science IQ Test

1. b	6. b
2. d	7. d
3. a	8. b
4. c	9. c
5. d	10. b

Give yourself one point for each correct answer and compute your total number of correct responses.

Total number correct _____

History IQ Test

1. b	6. c
2. b	7. c
3. b	8. c
4. a	9. d
5. a	10. d

Give yourself one point for each correct answer and compute your total number of correct responses.

Total number correct _____

Entertainment IQ Test

1. c	6. c
2. a	7. a
3. d	8. d
4. c	9. d
5. a	10. c

Give yourself one point for each correct answer and compute your total number of correct responses.

Total number correct _____

Food IQ Test

1. b	6. c
2. c	7. a
3. a	8. b
4. a	9. a
5. c	10. d

Give yourself one point for each correct answer and compute your total number of correct responses.

Total number correct _____

Sports IQ Test

1. b	6. a
2. c	7. c
3. d	8. a
4. b	9. d
5. b	10. b

Give yourself one point for each correct answer and compute your total number of correct responses.

Total number correct _____

Health IQ Test

1. c	6. d
2. d	7. d
3. c	8. a
4. c	9. d
5. d	10. a

Give yourself one point for each correct answer and compute your total number of correct responses.

Total number correct _____

Answers to Chapter 9

Children's Aptitude Test—3 to 6 years

1. c	6. d	11. b	16. d
2. d	7. d	12. d	17. c
3. c	8. c	13. d	18. d
4. d	9. d	14. b	19. c
5. b	10. c	15. a	20. c

Give your child one point for each correct answer. Then add the total number of correct responses.

Total number correct _____

Children's Aptitude Test—7 to 15 years

1. a	11. a	21. b	31. d
2. c	12. a	22. d	32. a
3. b	13. c	23. b	33. d
4. d	14. a	24. a	34. c
5. b	15. c	25. d	35. a
6. a	16. b	26. b	36. d
7. c	17. b	27. b	37. d
8. b	18. d	28. a	38. b
9. a	19. b	29. d	39. b
10. a	20. c	30. c	40. b

Give your child one point for each correct answer. Add the total correct.

Questions 1–20: Verbal test score _____

Questions 21–40: Nonverbal test score _____

Answers to Chapter 10

Hidden Gold

Answer: Door 1

Money Marbles

Answer: 41

4s and 9s

Answer: 4s. Explanation: There are many more 4s in the 40,000s. The 9s won't catch up until 90,000.

Students

1. Maria

2. 45. Explanation: 75% × 10% = 7.5% = 45

3. Tom

4. a and c

Socks and Clocks

1. a

2. 47. Explanation: Up to 46 he could still pull out two blue socks.

3. 1 out of 3

4. The one that's completely broken. It is right twice a day. The other clock is never right.

5. 2:40 P.M.

Buses and Planes

1. Simple. That is, if you know your own name.

2. 9,618

3. 1½ hours or 1 hour and 30 minutes or 90 minutes.

Fenced In

Answer: 71. If you said 72, remember, you need a post at the beginning and at the end of the fence.

Necessary Statements

1. b and c

2. b and d

Love Logic

Answer: a

Math-a-Logic

1. The complete addition works as follows: a = 2, b = 5, c = 4, d = 3, e = 1.

   25431

   32514

   12254

   + 24321

   ─────

   94,520

2. 167161

   664711

   162166

   + 164611

   1,158,649

3. 777 55555 6666666

Appendix B

Glossary

abstract reasoning   The ability to think on multiple levels and see relationships between ideas.

bell curve   Also called a "normal curve" or "normal distribution"; a graph that shows approximately how much of the population falls into each IQ range. In theory, if we tested everyone in the world with a traditional IQ test, most people would score in the average range. A smaller number would score moderately below average and moderately above average. Very high and very low scores are rare.

creativity   The ability to see many different possibilities or angles when solving a given problem. Creative persons can produce a product such as a work of art from their own resources and imagination with minimal instructions.

culture-fair IQ test   A test that uses nonverbal tasks to obtain a score that is independent of one's background, education, or language skills.

intelligence   The ability to learn about, learn from, understand, and interact with one's environment. This general ability consists of a number of specific abilities, including the following: adaptability to a new environment or to changes in the current environment; a capacity for knowledge and the ability to acquire it; a capacity for reason and abstract thought; the ability to comprehend relationships; the ability to evaluate and judge situations; and the capacity for original and productive thought.

intelligence quotient (IQ)   An indicator of a person's mental abilities relative to others of approximately the same age. An IQ score indicates specific mental abilities that can be measured accurately and are reliable predictors of academic and financial success.

learning disability   An inability to learn at a rate comparable to most members of a peer group due to lack of strength in a particular sense (e.g., vision) or area of the brain controlling that ability (e.g., the occipital area controls vision). A person with slight weakness in this area might learn better by hearing directions than by seeing a map.

long-term memory   The ability to retain learned information over a period of time and recall it as necessary.

Mensa International   The best-known high-IQ society that limits membership to those who score in the top 2 percent of a standardized test.

nonverbal score   Comprehension of pictures, patterns, spatial relationships, and visualizations that do not depend on language.

norms   A normative or mean score for a particular age group.

reliability   The likelihood that a test will produce similar results if administered at another time.

representative sample   A random sample of people that adequately represents the test-taking population in age, gender, race, and socioeconomic standing.

short-term memory   The ability to remember something for a limited period of time. This is also referred to as "working memory."

standard deviation   A measure of the distribution of scores around the average (mean). In a normal distribution, two standard deviations above and below the mean includes about 95 percent of all samples.

standardization   The process of determining established norms and procedures for a test to act as a standard reference point for future test results.

talent   The ability to do something especially well.

validity   The degree to which an IQ score predicts outcomes such as job performance, social functioning, or academic achievement.

verbal score   Comprehension of similar words or opposites, analogies, relationships, grammar, spelling, and language proficiency.

visualization   The ability to recall aspects of an object for the purpose of recreating it.

working memory   See *short-term memory*.

Appendix

Resources

Further Reading

American Psychological Association. *Report of a Task Force established by the Board of Scientific Affairs Intelligence: Knowns and Unknowns.* Washington, D.C., 1995.

Bryon, Mike. *Test Your IQ.* London: Kogan Page, 2002.

Cameron, Joseph. *IQ Challenge.* Memphis: Metro, 2001.

Carter, Philip. *Classic IQ Tests.* Memphis: Main Street, 2005.

———. *The Ultimate IQ Test Book: 1,000 Practice Test Questions to Boost Your Brain Power.* Memphis: Main Street, 2003.

Carter, Philip, and Kenneth Russell. *The Book of IQ Tests.* Memphis: Main Street, 2004.

Diamond, Marian, and Janet Hopson. *Magic Trees of the Mind: How to Nurture Your Child's Intelligence, Creativity, and Healthy Emotions from Birth through Adolescence.* New York: Plume, 1999.

Eysenck, Hans. *Test Your IQ*. New York: Penguin, 1996.

Gardner, Howard. *Frames of Mind: The Theory of Multiple Intelligences*. New York: Basic Books, 1999.

Gordon, Peter. *Match Wits with Mensa*. New York: Sterling, 2004.

Hercun, Deborah. *Improve Your IQ*. New York: Barnes and Noble, 1999.

———. *IQ and Human Intelligence*. New York: Oxford University Press, 1998.

Rimm, Sylvia. *Keys to Parenting the Gifted Child*. Hauppauge, NY: Barron's, 2001.

Russell, Ken. *Times Book of IQ Tests* (Book 5). London: Kogan Page, 2005.

Sigmond, Jola. *Visual IQ Tests*. New York: Sterling, 2004.

Sternberg, Robert, ed. *Why Smart People Can Be So Stupid*. New Haven: Yale University Press, 2002.

Sullivan, Norman. *The Big Book of IQ Tests*. New York: Black Dog & Leventhal, 1998.

Organizations

American Psychological Association (APA): 750 First St. NE, Washington, D.C. 20002–4242. (202) 336-5500. www.apa.org.

Council for Exceptional Children (CEC): The CEC is the largest international professional organization dedicated to improving educational outcomes for individuals with exceptionalities, students with disabilities, and/or the gifted. 1110 North Glebe Rd., Suite 300, Arlington, VA 22201. 1-888-232-7733. www.cec.sped.org.

Mensa International: Local listings worldwide. Mensa is the most famous high-IQ society in the world. 1-800-66-MENSA. www.mensa. org.

National Association for Gifted Children (NAGC): The NAGC is an organization of parents, teachers, educators, other professionals, and community leaders who unite to address the unique needs of children and youth with demonstrated gifts and talents as well as those children who may be able to develop their talents with appropriate educational experiences. Great Britain: 0845-450-0295. www.nagcbritain.org.uk.

National Center for Learning Disabilities (NCLD): The NCLD provides essential information to parents, professionals, and individuals with learning disabilities; promotes research and programs to foster effective learning; and advocates policies to protect and strengthen educational rights and opportunities. www.ncld.org.